Twelve Lessons

The Journal

By Kate Spencer

Published by Katherine Spencer Publishing

Copyright © Kate Spencer, 2016
All rights reserved

ISBN: 978-0-9934416-9-1
Paperback

From My Heart to Yours

For me, the biggest lesson of the last twelve months has to be Self-Care. I admit it - I initially thought that the whole concept was a bit lame. A social media status about "me time" made my skin crawl. I wanted to write sarcastic comments all over it about getting out there and making it happen instead of just "being".

I was a warrior of the light. A leader. A voice. Here to reach as many people as I could and help them to see their magnificence. I could work around the clock and juggle a million things. People said they didn't know how I managed to fit so much in. My ego patted me on the back and applauded. And then the inevitable. I crashed, and my superhero cape stopped flying and started tying me up in knots.

In the quest for looking after others, I'd given too much of myself. The drive to support, illuminate and help heal humanity had depleted me beyond belief. The energy reserves I had left were so pitiful they hardly fuelled the essentials of my day to day life. And I was forced to learn the lesson of looking after myself.

Physical exhaustion was just the initial heads up. The brink of emotional burn out was a scary place to be, and the loss of bandwidth and capacity to function was horrifying. Epiphany moments showed me that what I was sending out to the universe was that my time and energy were not worth protecting. And so I attracted in people and experiences that were a match to this. I had nothing much left to give and I had to withdraw. I had made myself too available, confusing this with the authenticity that I know I want to live and portray.

But I cannot be all things to all people, and neither can you. Big hearted me never wanted to turn anyone away that I could have helped. But in taking on everyone else's stuff I had stopped helping me, and the people I loved. The people who are important in my life deserve a version of me that can be present, patient, kind, funny and connected. And so do I.

I've had to be really honest with myself about what and who matters in my life, and make sure that myself and my own wellbeing are at the top of that list. I have had to assert much better boundaries and adopt a no drama policy as best I can. And above all I have had to know that this is not selfish at all, and that self-care is entirely my own responsibility, and it always will be. This experience has inspired me to write a chapter for you on something I call Tin Bucket Self Care, you'll see why when you read it.

As always, take what you need from my experience and my writing, and adapt, apply and dismiss as appropriate in your own life. My final words of wisdom on this are that the only thing that is lame about self-care, is thinking it's lame in the first place.

Love Kate x

How to Use this Book

You can read this book cover to cover, dip in and out as it suits, or ask the universe what is right for you to know right now and then open it at random. The Twelve Lessons Journal has been attracted into your experience because there is a vibrational match in some way, in other words there is something in here for you that will serve your greater good, don't ignore that.

Have a belief that you are getting what is meant for you in a given moment, suspend your ego and open your heart. After you have studied some or all of the lessons, you may want to get a little woo-woo and read about working with energy, rituals and the universe.

The Monthly Manifesting process of reviewing, releasing and renewing your focus will help you to stay clear about what you want to draw into your experience, and help you to stay aligned with receiving it.

There is plenty of space to doodle, write affirmations and notes and I encourage you to. Make this journal your sounding board, your daydream and your compass. There is great value in the journey back to you.

Love Kate x

"Promise me you'll always remember:
You're braver than you believe, and stronger than
you seem, and smarter than you think."

~ Christopher Robin to Pooh

www.kate-spencer.com

My gift to you...
Download your free meditation bundle here:
www.kate-spencer.com/the-journal-journey

LESSON 1

Be open to possibility

I AM open to
new possibilities;
I look at my
world with an
open mind and
create miracles in
every moment.

Lesson 1

The Phoenix ~ Be Open to Possibility

~ A Journey of a Thousand Miles begins with a Single Step ~ Lao Tzu

Often it takes a crisis or transition in life for us to open to the possibility that there could be more than our physical reality. There is an old adage that we don't know what we have until it's gone, and it is usually at a time of great loss or challenge we become open to considering the existence of a higher power, or even a miracle.

In these moments lessons can come thick and fast. They may be linked to unexpected change, relationships breaking down, illness, loss of a loved one or other circumstances that change your life significantly. They bring with them a type of re-evaluation and emotional stress.

I believe that for many of us, these moments can mark our *Awakening* to another way of living. A feeling of no longer worrying about 'the small stuff' can arise, as we shift our perception to things that are more valuable and important than possessions and work. Typically family becomes the main priority. Expressing how we feel, forgiving people, loving each other and fostering a faith that things will get better become important too.

It's the combination of the challenge and the pain, the struggle if you will, that I believe acts as the catalyst to bring up all of the universal questions that lie dormant within us as humans, waking up our consciousness.

Why me? Why now? What did I do to deserve this? Is there a bigger plan? How will I get through it? Where is my life going? Is there a God? Why am I here?

These questions and many more like them, come through as a prompt from our higher self, to start opening us up to the possibility that there is more to life as we know it. If you are a person who has previously only been able to believe what they can see, feel, hear, taste or touch then this could come as a massive revelation. Your human self may feel overwhelmed with the thought of these concepts initially.

Herein lies the first lesson – *Be Open to Possibility.*

This lesson is about having a more evolved perspective on life and events, suspending a critical and disbelieving nature and asking your ego to sidestep. There are concepts within this text that may push your buttons or make you scoff at times. Remember lesson one if this should happen and try to stay open. At the outset of *Twelve Lessons* the main character Stephanie has to start looking at her life via her higher self, rather than the ego and the human personality. Without lesson one Stephanie would not have been open to the journey ahead of her, and it is my greatest hope that if you are reading this book that you will be open to yours.

Stephanie's low self-worth had driven her to believe that she needed to buy friends and impress people in order to be liked, she bolstered her low self-esteem with expensive possessions in order for other people to deem her as 'worthy'. Trying to make people warm to her for what she had, rather than who she was. This is a trap that many of us find ourselves falling into in modern day living, materialism and low self-esteem can combine to create a destructive and vicious circle. This lesson asks you to look beyond the trappings of life as we know it, and strip back your beliefs about what you are worth as a person. Embrace the possibility that there is more than what you can see around you, know that you cannot measure your worth based on what you have, rather base it on who you are. Start to open to the thought that you are a soul that has chosen to come to earth at this time in order to grow, learn, experience and create.

Just as Stephanie's first lesson was to keep an open mind, I ask you to do the same. Please take a moment to set your intention that you are ready to receive new information and consider looking at your life in new ways. Work with your higher self and your intuition as you read this book and you will feel 'resonance' with certain chapters, phrases and lessons. This means they are striking a chord with you and that they mean something in your life at the moment. Your own personal guidance system is at work when you feel this, so take note. You may also find that different lessons and observations resonate differently at different times in your life. This is to be expected as we are all a work in progress.

The book you are reading was written with the love and intention to bring you the wisdom and insights that you can use to touch your life in enriching and nurturing ways. It's a reference and manifesto that will help you to work towards becoming the best version of yourself, and in turn create the best life that you can. All I ask of you now is that you allow yourself to *Be Open to Possibility*, and read on.

How could you open your mind and heart more to the possibility there is more?

Is there a part of you that is closed to things they can't see, touch or feel?

Are you ready to entertain the thought that new experiences and perspectives could be beneficial?

"I AM open to new possibilities; I look at my world with an open mind and create miracles in every moment."

LESSON 2

Self sabotage

I AM *releasing* all that is not in alignment with my greatest good now. I step into the light, it is my turn to shine.

Lesson 2

Shadow Self ~ Self-Sabotage

~It is not the mountain we conquer, but ourselves
~ Sir Edmund Hillary

As humans we are a vibrational combination of all of the thoughts, feelings, beliefs, emotions and experiences that we have ever encountered, in this lifetime and past incarnations. All of these factors are held in our energy system and guide our behaviour and decisions in our day to day lives. Sometimes they can be useful and empowering, but sometimes they sabotage us.

Your *Shadow Self* is the collection of all of these components created in your life which hold you back and sabotage you. It's the version of you that remembers all of the pain, mistakes, embarrassment and failure you have ever experienced throughout your whole existence—and it loves to remind you of them. We all have shadow aspects, and part of the journey towards living consciously is to heal the wounds and patterns of your *Shadow Self*. Do your best to see through illusions that your *Shadow Self* may project, and don't allow this aspect of you to control or influence your behaviour.

Let's see how easy it is for shadow aspects to form.

Imagine a scenario where a child is constantly compared to a sibling in a way that makes the child feel less worthy. This could be subtle or direct and may include undercurrents of comments such as the child's brother or sister being referred to as 'the pretty one' or 'the clever one'. It could be that there was a specific incident where the child made a mistake and was called stupid by an adult. This label was more than likely compounded by embarrassment and would lead to a core belief of "I am not good enough."

As this belief is integrated into the child's reality, it will start to taint or colour many things in their life and they are likely to start to adapt their behaviour in order to protect themselves against future rejection or exposure of 'not being good enough'. This may manifest as them not wanting to mix with new people, avoiding trying new sports or hobbies or not wanting to be in the school play. As the child gets older the consequences of having this core belief and programming will probably have an effect on academic performance, choice of peer group and relationships. They may be a loner and not have many friends, or may be part of a social group that treats them disrespectfully and as the butt of all jokes, and this child would be likely to allow this because deep down they feel 'not good enough'. They will not feel they deserve a better experience and will settle for what does not serve their highest good. This starts to become their *Shadow Self*.

If there was no intervention, as an adult, a version of this pattern could continue into choosing relationships that endorse the belief that they are 'not good enough' and they may end up being dominated and bullied. They would be likely to choose jobs they feel are safe and are probably underpaid with a lack of prospects—after all they are 'not good enough' for anything else and certainly outshone in many aspects of life.

This example is of course deliberately exaggerated and simplified, to illustrate how your personality can integrate information that does not serve you into your reality. It also shows how this can grow in your consciousness to become something that dominates you and your life choices. You may find that with introspection, you discover parts of your shadow that have been steering your behaviour for years, perhaps most of your life. Becoming conscious of these parts is the first step to healing them and overcoming their influence.

Most of the time the information that we have gathered in order to form these shadow aspects is either someone else's unconscious opinion, or it's actually not true at all. Think again about the child that was called "stupid", but consider different contexts that could apply to the situation. Was the child doing something that was actually stupid and the adult meant the behaviour was stupid but not the child? Or perhaps this was an adult that had no idea of the insensitivity of saying the word 'stupid'. It may have had a different meaning for them and not had anything like the gravity it had for the child. A throwaway comment became a belief that the child then formed about themselves. The way we form beliefs depends on the meaning that we give information at a given time, and sometimes due to past experiences, expectations, context and personalities we get this wrong.

You may find you have been carrying around a shadow part of yourself for years based on something that you got totally wrong in the first place and you have allowed this illusion to influence the choices that you have made.

It's time to free yourself from your shadow and the self-sabotage that it could be creating in your life. Release the old beliefs that do not serve you and step into the light where shadows don't exist.

Which beliefs do you hold about yourself that sabotage you?

When and how were these beliefs formed?

What would your life look like if you didn't live through this shadow part of yourself?

"I AM releasing all that is not in alignment with my greatest good now. I step into the light, it is my turn to shine."

LESSON 3

You attract
what you are

I AM attracting
all things good
into my life.

Lesson 3

Attraction ~ You Attract What You Are

> ~ You live in a vibrational universe, you can control the signal you emit ~ Esther Hicks

We live in a vibrational universe. Everything has a frequency or energy vibration including physical objects, thoughts and feelings. As a human being you are a combination of many different vibrations all combined together to create your own unique energetic signature, like a vibrational fingerprint.

The interesting thing about this is that your signature is magnetic and, like all energy, it attracts like for like frequencies to it from out there in the universe. *You Attract What You Are*, and you will have seen evidence for this when you start to focus your (magnetic) thoughts on to something like a new car. Suddenly you start to draw to you lots of examples of the car that you are focused on in different situations such as television adverts, actual examples of the car and overhearing conversations about it. Here lies the power of attraction.

This is a mind-blowing concept, and even more amazing is that we have the power to change our energy vibration and deliberately bring it into alignment with things and experiences that we want to draw to us into our lives. This is the art of manifestation and is rooted in quantum physics. There is much research to show we can influence future possibilities by changing our thoughts, intentions and feelings, which in turn change our energy vibration and attraction field.

It is important to stay conscious about what you are thinking and feeling, in order to draw to you what you want instead of what you don't. You can work with *The Law of Attraction* to help create your life experience and to literally magnetise to you what you want.

The first step is to become an observer of your own mind. Step back and see what thoughts and feelings are moving through you, and then understand these are triggering an energy vibration or magnetic field around you that will attract like for like frequencies. This means taking responsibility for what you have in your life now, knowing that there was an energetic participation by you at some stage, what you have now is a result of how you have felt and believed in the past.

Once you have started to see which thoughts, beliefs and feelings are playing out for you in your life, you can make a decision to consciously change them. The phrase "thoughts become things" is true in all aspects of our lives. This concept has massive ramifications. What if we could actually change real life outcomes by changing our thoughts? Instead of living reactively to whatever life brings you on a daily basis, could there possibly be a way of consciously creating?

When I first found out about *The Law of Attraction* I was curious but sceptical, but since then I have used it to great effect. In fact the book you are reading now and the novel *Twelve Lessons* were brought into publication with a huge amount of help from *The Law of Attraction*. After about twenty rejections from publishers, my faith began waning. I was feeling like it was never going to happen for me and although I loved *Twelve Lessons*, maybe it was not going to reach the millions of people that I had hoped it would. The more I got stuck in this cycle of thinking, the less positive results I had and eventually I pushed the manuscript and enquiry letters into a carrier bag and under my bed. I went back to my day to day life and resigned myself to the fact that I had been unrealistic about ever being published.

It was at this time I shared my feelings with my biggest supporter, my sister Emma who pointed out the obvious.

"Of course it's not happening, you don't believe it anymore, you've lost faith."

The penny dropped that it was time now to dig deep, change my thinking. No wonder I was experiencing rejection, if *You Attract What You Are* my thoughts were now focused on my dream being stopped in its tracks. After some introspection and inner work I started to change my perception of the situation.

I shifted my focus to drawing in the *right* person that would help me to publish my book and help me to help millions of people worldwide. I started to use affirmations about this and visualise that the right person was there in my life and that they loved *Twelve Lessons* as much as I did, they could see my big vision and they were excited about it too.

Sometimes when you are using *The Law of Attraction* to create an experience, the universe can join the dots up in unexpected ways. Until now I had kept *Twelve Lessons* a secret. I was afraid of failure and people judging me for writing a book that had not achieved publication. Again my sister and wise friend spoke to me about this and asked me what my goal had been when I was writing. I thought for a moment and realised that ultimately I wanted to share a funny and touching story of a believable character that people could relate to, in order to deliver universal lessons that would serve them in their lives. And since I had a copy of the first draft on my laptop, and a couple of copies stuffed under my bed, there was actually nothing stopping me from doing just that.

I had to get out of the thought process of "my book is never going to reach people" and into the energy of "people love my book, it's helping them and entertaining them," and I took a bold step by giving it to my dance teacher, Nicola Oliver. I was in transition at this time and still in fear of rejection, so I only gave her the first few pages to see what she thought. She sent me a text within the hour demanding more and I ran around the corner in the dark and pushed the remaining chapters through her letterbox! My emotions flipped from doom and gloom to hope, excitement and elation that 'people liked my book' and this was the energy I found myself in. Nicola devoured *Twelve Lessons* within forty eight hours and, completely unbeknown to me, passed it on to her colleague and our mutual friend Jill Newton. When she told me this I panicked but stepped back from the drama and realised that she had passed it on for two reasons, firstly she loved it and secondly I was manifesting great things for *Twelve Lessons* and in order for it to be a success I had to be in a good energetic vibration about it. The universe was joining up the dots for me to help create my vision. Jill loved my work and again, passed it on.

Before I knew it news started to spread about *Twelve Lessons* and how it was touching people's lives; I even had to start a waiting list as word spread like wildfire onto friends, neighbours and the school yard. People were having conversations about my book and I started overhearing the odd snippet here and there, I was thrilled to hear my characters and plot discussed on street corners and even in the supermarket. Every now and then someone would ask if they could pass it on to a friend and jump the waiting list because "they really need to read it Kate…!"

There were soon three different carrier bags containing a full copy each printed out on A4 paper being circulated. Reams of paper started to show up on my doorstep with stuck on post-it notes and scribbled requests, I could hardly believe that there was such a demand. It was in the midst of this amazing energy that I started to truly believe I could have what I wanted. For the first time I could actually see my dream as a reality. The stories about how *Twelve Lessons* was changing lives and waking people up to a new way of looking at themselves were astonishing and humbling. The book was doing what I had intended and I was in gratitude, even if it was only changing hands in a carrier bag, *Twelve Lessons* was a success.

It was around this time that the universe joined up the dots for me and sent me my publisher Maria, whilst I was firmly in the energy and thought pattern of 'my book is amazing and it's reaching lots of people'.

I will always be grateful to my precious friends Nicola Oliver and Jill Newton for loving *Twelve Lessons* and passing it on without telling me! They both did me the most amazing kindness, they were touched by my writing and had confidence it is when mine was struggling. They helped to bring my work into the lives of many people, to reach them, teach them and support them on their journey, from carrier bag to book shelf thanks to two amazing ladies.

And now my writing and message has come your way too. I believe that when we draw a book towards us there is something in it that is in resonance with us, and it is my intention that both this companion guide and *Twelve Lessons* resonate with many and help them on their journey, you included.

My journey to publication is a great example of *You Attract What You Are*.

Become conscious of what you are sending out there energetically and bring in more of what you want into your life.

What are you attracting into your life at the moment?

What would you like to change about this?

What can you do with your own thinking to change your experience?

"I AM attracting all things good into my life."

"May your choices reflect your hopes, not your fears."

~ Nelson Mandela

LESSON 4

Release what does not serve you

I AM releasing
what does
not serve me
now with grace
and ease.

Lesson 4

The Web ~ Old Stuff Keeps You Stuck

~ Be willing to surrender what you are for what you could become ~ Mahatma Gandhi

All objects, thoughts, feelings, people, animals, plants and buildings have a different energy vibration. Take a moment now to look around the space you are in now, and consider all of the different energetic frequencies that surround you. Then factor yourself into the mix as well, and the complexity of your unique human vibration. It is the combined result of these energetic signals that create the 'feeling' of a place or person. There are also other influences such as light, sound, earth energies and other people.

Cluttered and busy energy can make you feel overwhelmed or stressed, whilst clear energy creates calm. If your environment is filled with things that you no longer want or need, or things that have a negative association or emotion attached to them from your past, then this will drain you of positive energy and affect you detrimentally.

Imagine you have hoarded 'thin' clothes in case you slim into them and the truth of the situation is you are a voluptuous size sixteen or more and that you couldn't get a pair of skinny jeans over your thighs, never mind your backside (yes this is the voice of experience!). How do you feel when you look at these 'thin' clothes? If they are really motivating you to eat well and exercise regularly and you are heading towards your goal weight as a result, then keep them. On the other hand if they make you feel like a monumental failure every time you open your wardrobe and your heart sinks, wishing that you could reclaim your size twelve figure, then this is not helpful. Remember that the way you feel contributes to your field of attraction and manifests experiences into your life that match the energy of your emotions. If you are going to start your day with a feeling that vibrates 'I am a fat failure' then your life is going to reflect that and you will not make the progress you deserve. You will then be likely to associate even more negative feelings with the 'thin clothes' and create an ongoing vibration that will not serve you. My advice is to give these clothes to a charity shop or friend and set yourself free from the old energy. This will lift and change your vibration immediately and by feeling better you will start to attract better experiences to you.

Old stuff can also be the personal stuff you are carrying around with you in terms of memories, experiences, relationships, friendships, obligations, worries and beliefs. Sometimes this can be a literal release such as passing on physical items or throwing them away, or even a more radical release like moving house or changing a job.

When it comes to relationships this can be more challenging. Sometimes we know that a relationship has reached its end and that the best course of action is to release this with sensitivity towards both parties. This is a journey in itself and would fill a whole other book. There are circumstances however where relationships *as they are currently* do not serve us, but by changing boundaries, communication, arrangements and perceptions there is the possibility of reaching a new level that serves both parties.

This can release negativity, unrealistic expectations and tension between you and other people, and in this case you can view the *Old Stuff* as old patterns in the relationship that were not working. A useful and practical way to move *Old Stuff* out of your life and energy field is to write it down with the intention of clearing the issue, relationship or painful memory and then burn this and ask the universe to transmute this into love and light. You can also write letters to individual people either in your life now or from your past, with the intention of setting you both free from a negative situation and then follow the same procedure.

As you change your own internal reality and start to shift, you will find that you feel the urge to start to clear up your life as you knew it. What no longer serves you will naturally start to move out of your life, as you align your thoughts and feelings up with healing, enlightenment, spiritual progress and living more consciously. The universe will support this and seemingly random events will start to occur in to help you towards your goals. Friends will ask if you have something they need, you will be asked to donate jumble, you will be inspired to de-clutter and have a car boot sale or maybe list old items on *eBay*. People that you found really hard work and negative in nature will move away, disconnect from you or move out of your circle. This is your own energy drawing in change in your life experience. There is a natural drifting out of *Old Stuff* to make space for the new people and experiences that you will attract that will be more aligned with who you are becoming.

Old Stuff Keeps You Stuck, so find out what your old stuff is and a way to let it go.

What are you hanging on to that you need to release?

Why are you hanging on to this?

What would your life look and feel like if you could set yourself free and let go?

"I AM releasing what does not serve me now with grace and ease."

LESSON 5

You are a creator

I AM consciously creating a magnificent life experience for myself now.

Lesson 5

Universal Magic ~ You Are a Creator

~ Life is not happening to you, it's responding to you ~ Rhonda Byrne

This lesson is an expansion of lesson three, *You Attract What You Are*. You now know the universe is responding to all of the thoughts, feelings, emotions and energies that are combined to make up you, and that this frequency draws in 'like for like' energies and experiences. This means that *You Are a Creator* of your life thought by thought, feeling by feeling and moment by moment. There may be parts of you that feel uncomfortable with this and want to challenge the very idea. This is normal and is usually a part of you that is stuck, and is creating resistance. If you find this happening, and you start to get some internal chatter about this concept not being right, pause for a moment and breathe. Tell yourself this is a thought that does not serve you and that you honour it, but you are choosing to think differently now.

Once you are in a place on your own journey where you are ready to take responsibility for what you are creating in your life, you can make the transition and become a *conscious* creator. This means that you can change the way you are thinking and feeling in order to deliberately send out specific vibrations to attract specific outcomes. This takes practice and at first can feel fake, but there is truth in the old saying 'fake it until you make it'.

Affirmations can be really useful and can help to programme your mind to shift your perception and your vibration, you will have seen that I have written some for each lesson to get you started. The work of *Louise Hay* highlighted their importance in her truly amazing and timeless book *You Can Heal Your Life*. Affirmations are statements you can say out loud or silently in your own mind that affirm an idea or concept, and as such start to move your attraction field to be more in alignment with what you want to create. Affirmations must be positive and in the present tense, remember *You Attract What You Are,* so you need to trigger the feeling and therefore the vibration in the current now time in order to create what you want and draw it in.

When you find yourself in a holding pattern in your life where circumstances keep repeating, or a situation that you want to change, firstly take a step back from your own mind and examine your thinking. Write down the phrases and words that you would generally use about this and have a look at how you are drawing in more like for like energy. For example, if you are a person that says or thinks "I am always tired" then there is little likelihood that you will be attracting more energy any day soon. Likewise "I've never got any money" or "He doesn't understand me" would create similarly unhelpful energetic patterns for you in your life in relation to finances and relationships.

Once you have found the phrases and thinking patterns that are keeping you stuck, write them down. Now join up the dots between what you have been thinking and what you have been getting, and it should be obvious, if you have been honest, why you have been stuck or missing out on what you want.

You should clearly see the link between your thoughts and what you are drawing in, and if you don't at this stage, then start to use some affirmations about having clarity and being able to easily see what you need to in order to make progress. After a day or two of affirming this you will find that you can return to this exercise with a different perspective.

Next take a moment to think about what it is you *do* want to experience. Let this run through your mind as a conscious experience and start to think of some powerful, positive and present tense affirmations to support this. Write them as if this happening right now, not in the future. Use empowering and inspiring language that makes you feel good. Don't allow your ego to start butting in and say that you can't have what you are asking for, and don't worry about how it's going to happen either. Create your affirmations and start using them in order to start drawing in the change you want. Visualisation really helps when you are saying affirmations, it makes it easier to get into alignment energetically. If you are a person that struggles with this consider making a vision board or a vision book. Look for pictures and representations of what it is that you want to create and start to collate a mosaic of all of the things you desire. This can of course be a work in progress, and as you change your desire you can change the content.

Look at this regularly and affirm at the same time. Some affirmation examples could be:

"I am blessed with an abundance of health, wealth and happiness."

"I love myself unconditionally and my life reflects this back to me."

"Money and opportunity flow to me easily at all times, I always have more than I need."

"My life is full of strong and healthy relationships."

"My body is strong and healthy."

Although you are now on a journey to live more consciously, many people in the world today are living unconsciously and would not accept the idea that *You Are a Creator.* They are on a type of human autopilot, going through their routine, day in day out and not necessarily being aware of their own thoughts, feelings and vibration. They may have a tendency to be influenced by other ideas that are not their own, such as the media or other people's opinions, and they may take little responsibility for what is being created in their lives.

These are the people who blame society, the government, their spouse, and anyone else for the way that their life is turning out, they would rarely look within themselves in order to make positive change. When living life unconsciously, it's easy to think that someone else should save you and people with this lack of awareness can end up having quite a self-orientated outlook on life. There is often a sense of entitlement with people who are living very unconsciously and they can find it challenging to be happy for other people's success, as they often feel that life is unfair to them so why should others have what they want. This is a pattern and a way of living that keeps you stuck and, as we know, will attract more and more of the same energy to them until they change the way they look at life. In this case their beliefs and attitude are the *Old Stuff* that they need to work on releasing. None of this is said in judgment; there is a difference between this and observation.

It's important to add here that just because you are awake and setting your intention to live consciously, you are no better than anyone else. All of us have equal opportunity to awaken and live consciously and some choose it whilst some don't. It is not your job to go around trying to get people to see things from your point of view or to rescue them into enlightenment. This would come from a place of ego as if you were living in a way that was superior to them, and this is not the case. You may be observing characteristics in these people who are living unconsciously that are being brought to you by *The Law of Reflection,* showing you aspects of yourself that you still need to work on. You may even have soul contracts with someone that they will not awaken in this life time in order to be able to share lessons with you that will accelerate your own progress.

Honour everyone's journey and do not fall into the trap of being in judgment, we are all where we are meant to be at this time and we are all equal and doing our own version of our best. Sometimes we need to be able to see the contrast in life in order to know what we want, and now that you know *You Are a Creator* this will be valuable to you.

Living your life as a conscious creator and being in your truth will provide reflections for others. This may draw to you opportunities to signpost people and talk to them about ideas you have applied to your own life, and pass on information. As long as this is done with the intention of supporting and not fixing, the exchange will have the energy of service rather than control. You will also have to let go of the outcome and realise that we all have our own free will. You may have planted a seed that will be nurtured for a while before it starts to grow. This all depends on each individuals desire to grow and change their perception and work towards overcoming their own limitations.

You Are a Creator of your own life experience, embrace this concept and draw in what you desire.

What are you choosing to create in your life right now?

What frequency do you need to send out to the universe to create this?

What do you need to release in order to generate this frequency?

"I AM consciously creating a magnificent life experience for myself now."

"Dear Karma, I have a list of the people you missed."

~ Unknown

LESSON 6

❧

The law of karma

I AM releasing all vows, oaths, contracts, binds and agreements that are karmic in nature that I am ready to resolve now.

Lesson 6

The Law of Karma ~ Cause & Effect

*~ There are the waves and there is the wind, seen
and unseen forces. Everyone has these same
elements in their lives, the seen and the unseen,
karma and free will ~ Kuan Yin*

"I must have been wicked in a past life," is something
that people say, usually when their circumstances are less
than perfect in their current situation. Although a
throwaway comment, there is some truth in this statement
and there is a universal *Law of Karma* that plays out for
all of us.

An easy way to understand this concept is the idea of
Cause and Effect, the age old principle that whatever you
give out you will get back at some stage, in this life time
or another.

As a past-life regressionist, I believe in past lives and the
imprints they leave in the fabric of your soul, as well as
the karma and the contracts that they imbue. I have helped
and supported people who have had physical symptoms in
this lifetime, emotional responses, fears and phobias or
relationship issues to release and heal the cause of these
through their past lives, and create massive change in their
current life. Under hypnosis they describe how they have
often chosen to incarnate with the same souls again, as
part of a soul group in order to resolve karma and pay
back karmic debts that were created in other times and
places. These members of your soul group usually

represent friends and family or key people in your life here on earth, and *The Law of Karma* can often highlight why we experience such dramatic life lessons and challenges in close relationships at times.

It's important to add that you cannot 'clear' karma unless someone has worked through it and understood the underlying lesson and reason behind it. Karma can be quick and come back to you almost immediately, or it can take weeks, years or lifetimes. Sometimes it is necessary to go back to the initial experience or incident either with the help of a practitioner or yourself in a meditation or reflective state, and to consciously look at the lesson in order to release it. You can find that there is some sort of specific action you need to take—for example breaking a vow or agreement, exercising forgiveness or offering an apology.

Knowing about the existence of karma and understanding it can mean that you change the way you are living your life and can help you towards being more conscious and considerate. No thought, action, word or deed goes unnoticed by the universe and the *Law of Karma*, it's all recorded in your soul or Akashic Records.

The returning of your karma may not be an exact replica of the energy you sent out there in the first place, but there is nearly always an association. For example, if you are a person who pokes fun at other people and has a critical attitude you may find that the universe interprets this as you taking away the self-confidence of others. In terms of karma you may find there is an incident of random identity fraud that means money is stolen from your back account. This is the universe taking from you and also affecting your worth, therein lies the association. Each example is completely individual and therefore trust your own intuition and gut feeling about what is playing out in your own life, it's been framed up this way so that you can recognise the lessons and grow.

Interpretation is as individual as the lesson itself, so if you do seek guidance from a practitioner make sure that you only take what resonates with you. We must all remember that even the best psychics, readers and healers are here in a human body and as such they are filtering information through their own brain, belief system, ego and personality. So if they say something that you feel in your own intuition is not right for you, then empower yourself and don't take this on board.

Past Life or Spiritual regression can be very useful because this process will help you to channel the information that you need when in an altered state, so it will come directly from your higher self and will not be filtered through someone else. A skilled practitioner will not lead you with their questioning and will facilitate but not influence what you are receiving through. Karma can be released this way.

Another important thing to note about karma is that it repeats until it is resolved. If you have a karmic lesson coming up in your life, you will find it manifests in different guises over and over until you recognise the essence of the lesson, or experience that you need to learn, resolve and release. It's often a clue in your life that you have something karmic playing out when you keep drawing in situations and people that bring the same type of challenge. Even though you have worked on your energy and consciousness to change your resonance to these, you may find that they are still attracted into your life because of the karmic link that you have not as yet resolved and that *Cause and Effect* is playing out. You may find that you keep bringing experiencing a circumstance or type of person over and over again and you don't know why things seem to keep turning out the same way, even though there are different players on the stage and there is a different setting. This is another clue for you that there could be karma involved.

You may find that through your meditation, intuition or work with a practitioner you have made vows and agreements in past lives that are still active in this life. An example would be if you have been married before and vowed and promised yourself to one person and then find that this overshadows your current life relationship, or perhaps you have taken vows of poverty as part of a religion or spiritual ceremony. These really can have a knock on effect in your life now, and once they have been identified on a conscious level and the time comes to release them you can use this affirmation:

"By divine decree and in the name of my God Presence I AM, I now break any and all vows, oaths, covenants, agreements, contracts and binds in relation to (insert name or situation) that I am ready to release from my consciousness, energy body, cell memories and karmic records now."

Hold the intention that you are asking for a dispensation because you have learned what is it that you needed to experience, and that you are in gratitude for this and also for the release and resolution. You may need to use the affirmation several times if the karma is multi-faceted and change the wording each time, for example this could be about a relationship breakdown but might also affect finances and your self-confidence. *The Law of Karma* can also return goodness into your life that you have sent out in the past, it doesn't all have to challenging or negative. And the good thing about this is that when you live consciously you can look for opportunities to practice kindness, gratitude, forgiveness, grace and much more, that will help towards your future karma in either this life or the next. Be mindful of the concept of *Cause and Effect*, and start banking good karma that will be returned when the time is right.

What are the repeating lessons and experiences in your life that you feel could be karmic?

What do you need to work on, learn or release in order to resolve this?

Are you ready to do this work now or do you need to wait for a time in the future?

"I AM releasing all vows, contracts, oaths, contracts, binds and agreements that are karmic in nature that I am ready to resolve now."

LESSON 7

The law of reflection

I AM *embracing*
the reflections that
life is bringing me
and in gratitude
for the opportunity
to grow.

Lesson 7

Mirror, Mirror ~ The Law of Reflection

~ The good we find in others, is in you too. The faults you find in others are your faults as well. After all to recognise something you must know it ~ Unknown

The *Law of Reflection* states that life is a mirror and literally reflects back to us a version of our self in order to highlight and illuminate our attributes and flaws. This process shows us through people, situations and experiences that are drawn to us, what is really going on with us.

Sometimes reflections are subtle and sometimes they are blatantly obvious. This can depend on lots of things such as how badly the universe wants to bring the reflection to your attention for your growth and development, and perhaps how many times you have missed the reflection in the past. In my experience reflections are often highlighted to us by the use of emotional triggers, which can make us feel uncomfortable, upset, angry or irritated with a person or situation. When you feel this way, take a step back and ask yourself what *The Law of Reflection* wants you to see.

One of the easiest ways for the human mind to work with reflections is to view your life as a play being staged on the earth. See each person in your circle as an actor that has a part to play in helping you to grow spiritually and personally, and to expand your consciousness. This way you can start to be in gratitude for reflections and not get tied up in anger, resentment, judgment or a lack of personal responsibility.

Our greatest teachers bring us the most challenging reflections. It is of course far easier to ignore *The Law of Reflection* and instead blame others for not being enlightened or awake. When you are ready to work with reflections you will find that although challenging at times, that the gift of growth and self-realisation that you receive is definitely worth it.

The traits and examples that *The Law of Reflection* brings you will show you an aspect of your own consciousness to a lesser or greater degree. There may not be a literal translation here, so look for the essence that is being highlighted to you, this may take some time and introspection. Like with Karma you may not get the exact information that gives you the exact match and detail you want. You will need to be open and use your intuition to see what each reflection means to you, and how it serves you in a given moment. Start to view reflections as gifts, and the harder they are to swallow the greater the gift and the greater the shortcut to your own development and enlightenment.

Once you are consciously aware that reflections are occurring in your life, you will become more tuned into them and feel the difference between a reflection and a random day to day occurrence. It would be contaminating, draining and tiring to go through every day of your life reading 'the reflections' into every single interaction and event. Instead know that you are open to working with *The Law of Reflection* in order to better yourself, and then look for a gut feeling or emotional response to a person or event. Step back from this and pause for a moment, and ask for the essence of the reflection. It might come to you as a thought, feeling, knowing or realisation, or you may need to get some distance and meditate on this. Once you have the reflection it's time for you to take an honest look at the patterns and beliefs, relationships, behaviour and traits that do not serve you and how the reflection matches up. Now you are conscious of this, you need to do your own inner work in order to change.

You will know if the changes that you have made have been effective, because the universe no longer needs to highlight this information to you. Reflections of this particular nature will stop or wane and you will no longer attract (through *Law of Attraction*) the same, people and situations.

In other words you will stop bringing to you what was being brought to highlight your old patterns. Once the pattern has gone there will no longer be resonance and nothing to bring to your attention through *The Law of Reflection.*

What reflections are you seeing in others that make you feel irritated, uncomfortable and upset?

Which repeating reflections have you been given by different people and situations?

Which thought, feeling or behaviour pattern do you need to release in order to stop attracting these reflections?

"I AM embracing the reflections that life is bringing me and in gratitude for the opportunity to grow."

LESSON 8

Compassion
and forgiveness

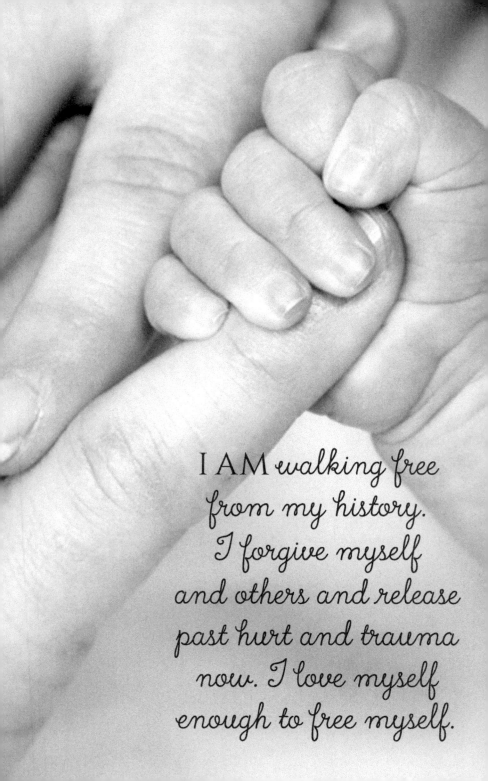

I AM walking free from my history. I forgive myself and others and release past hurt and trauma now. I love myself enough to free myself.

Lesson 8

Forgiveness & Compassion

~ Forgiveness is the fragrance that the violet sheds on the heel that has crushed it ~ Mark Twain

Forgiveness is an active process. It's not something that just magically happens over time, you need to be a willing spirit and an active participant to allow forgiveness, and you need to choose it for yourself. By keeping yourself bound to anger, resentment and hurt in the past you are chaining only you and not those people or situations that you feel wronged by.

Many of us have had experiences in our past where we have suffered in some way, physically, emotionally, financially, mentally or otherwise. These experiences can leave deep and lasting scars within us and can fuel feelings of anger and pain for a long time after the initial event, and sometimes even a lifetime.

As humans there is a tendency sometimes to slip into victim mode and gain some sort of satisfaction from rehashing the story of events, telling people how you were hard done by. When you are living consciously it's important to see that your ego is at times thriving on this, but that in truth you are stuck in a pattern that is holding you back and creating resistance in your life. By going over the story and holding on to the anger and resentment you are keeping active the feelings and vibrations in your energy system and this can lead to physical symptoms in your body and disease over the long term. This stops you from being in the allowing space that lets energy flow easily into your life to bring you goodness and joy.

We have already established that *You Attract What You Are*. With this in mind, you can clearly see what the universe will send you if part of your core signature vibration is sending out energy that says, "I am a victim, I am treated really badly by life and people, poor me." You will get more of the same and this will confirm to your ego that yes indeed you are a victim, and that life dealt you a really bad hand this time round. The life of your dreams will be kept totally out of your reach and you will contaminate relationships, opportunities and experiences time after time. This is self-sabotage in action.

I know that there will be people reading this right now that think I don't understand just how bad they have had it. Maybe I have not had exactly the experience that you have had, but like all of us I have walked my own journey and there have been many opportunities to practice forgiveness and compassion. There have also been times that I have really struggled and my victim mode has firmly kicked in, as I wanted to rant and rave and hold on to fury and revenge that has surged through me. Like you I am a work in progress. If you have feelings of 'poor me' coming up as you are reading this, know that there is definitely something really important for you within this lesson.

I have found in my experience of forgiveness and compassion, that it is useful to foster the belief that every single person is doing the best that they can in any given moment in life. Each one of us is here in a human body going through our own experiences and attracting what is in resonance with us at that time. Some people are awake to living consciously and some are not. We have all had different childhoods, parental input (or not), incomes, siblings, schooling, interactions, experiences and histories. All of these different aspects and many more have combined to make us the version of ourselves that walks the earth today, and the same can be said for everyone else.

It's from this unique place of 'who we are' that we make decisions and take action, and as individuals we all see things and process things differently depending on 'who we are.'

If we are all doing the best that we can based on who we are, then this version of best will be different for us all, and other people's reactions, opinions and behaviour will not always align with ours.

Even when people hurt us they are doing the best that they can based on who they are. When we are on the receiving end of this it's not easy to see things this way, and sometimes we need time and distance to be able to disconnect enough from the raw feelings to be able to process this.

Look past the behaviour and know that this is a playing out of someone else's internal struggle or fear, and although it may feel like it's personal in the moment, it's not actually your stuff at all.

By hanging on to what has happened to you in the past you are asking through your energy system to stay stuck and accept more of these feelings and experiences in the future. You cannot receive what is coming into your life in terms of goodness and joy if your hands are full of your *Old Stuff,* which could be anger and resentment.

Simply put, if someone wronged you twenty years ago, and you have carried around that pain and resentment for all of this time, there is only one thing worse than that. Twenty years and one more day. Exercise *Forgiveness and Compassion* and set yourself free.

Who and what do you need to forgive in your life?

Which feelings and experiences might you be hanging on to and rehashing in order to fuel your inner victim and ego?

What do you need to do in order to free yourself?

"I AM walking free from my history. I forgive myself and others and release past hurt and trauma now. I love myself enough to free myself."

"Healing your wounds, living consciously and showing up in your own life are three of the most powerful things you can do to help yourself and everyone else."

~ Kate Spencer

LESSON 9

~ ❧ ~

You can't fix other people

I AM responsible for myself and my own journey. I can support other souls without being in judgement or trying to fix anyone. We are all equal and where we should be on our own life path.

Lesson 9

Acceptance ~ You Can't Fix Other People

~ You are your own best chance, and that goes for all of us ~ Kate Spencer

You will find that as you transition and move into a life that is more conscious, that you will look back on your old way of thinking and being and see that there truly was a time when you experienced an *Awakening*.

It is upon awakening that we become hungry for information and knowledge. You will seek out books, websites and resources that can start to sign post you towards a whole new and vast subject of consciousness, attraction, healing and enlightenment. As you learn more you will find that your experience of life will change in positive ways. You will start to learn spiritual and soul lessons and align with your greatest and highest good. Over time you will adopt a more 'higher self' perspective on life and lower vibration emotions such as jealousy, anger and hate will not be with you for long periods, if at all.

My awakening was both rapid and profound and it felt from that a world that had been in black and white my whole life was suddenly in glorious Technicolor. I armed myself with all of the new information I'd found, and set out to rescue as many people as I could. I believed that this had to be my mission in life and I was going to fulfil it no matter what. People needed to wake up and I was just the person to help them. Thank God I'd arrived!

What I didn't realise at this early stage was that the more people I tried to save and rescue, the thicker and faster the reflections and lessons came in for me! And I wasn't ready to notice them one bit. My ego blamed everyone else for being so negative and totally missed the point that the real lesson here was that I couldn't fix anyone else and I only had responsibility for my own journey. All of these people were doing me a great service by rebuffing my attempts and turning their back on my message, in doing so that they were giving me the real message that I needed to see - *You Can't Fix Other People*. Cosmic irony that I was not prepared to accept. The truth is, people awaken when they are ready, and some never will.

That however is no one else's responsibility; it lies entirely with that individual. There may have been soul contracts made by some to not awaken in this lifetime, in order to experience certain lessons or feelings that will help them to grow. They may have agreed to help others to experience lessons or reflections in order to expand their consciousness. For instance someone may be living a life that we consider to be inappropriate or dark in some way, but they may have agreed before coming to earth to do this to help others to work on judgment issues. Therefore there is nobility in their cause and we should not allow our ego to push us into arrogance and feel superior.

You will know if you have slipped into 'fixing' mode with others or judgment because life will start to match this up vibrationally and send you people that react this way to you. Instead of getting annoyed, thank the universe for the reflection and go within, ask yourself who you have tried to fix or been in judgment of and how you can release this. It is especially important if you are working as a healer or a therapist, holding the intention that you are there to help and support people to help themselves, rather than you fixing them is very important. If you are coming from a place of being able to fix people then you will attract people who are unwilling to take responsibility for their own healing and progress and this could end up in a whole lot of different scenarios. They may blame you for not helping them, or they may keep returning time after time for the same or similar issues and leave you frustrated and drained. Make sure you let people know that you are a catalyst for their *own* change, a support to their *own* healing and transformation. This will empower you both and often means that the healing is more profound and happens quicker.

You may find that as you live a more conscious life and your resonance changes, that you don't feel as much of a connection with some of the people and situations in your life as you once did. When you awaken and during your spiritual journey your energy signature or vibration will change. This means that there can be less resonance or attraction between you and what used to feel right. If you have had a dramatic shift in your vibration you may find that you suddenly experience energetic dissonance between you and some others, this can feel like a type of repelling when you are in their company. You may find that you experience irritation, anger and resentment more readily than before.

It's important to know that when this happens it's perfectly all right to allow relationships to start to drift or evolve to a different way of relating that gives you more space to be the newer version of you, as discussed in the lesson *Old Stuff Keeps You Stuck*. You may find that situations such as your place of employment or family gatherings start to feel challenging for you as there may be less resonance now. Know that *You Can't Fix Other People* and find a way to relax in your own self, knowing that you are doing what is right for you and so are they. Part of your evolution will be to attract more people that are in resonance with you. Your peer group may change as a result of your new experiences, don't resist this, hold the intention that all is well and things are unfolding as they should be. Focus on your own inner work and know that *You Can't Fix Other People.*

Who have you been trying to fix?

Why do you feel the need to fix them?

How are you going to work on yourself to stop being a fixer?

"I AM responsible for myself and my own journey. I can support other souls without being in judgement or trying to fix anyone. We are all equal and where we should be on our own life path."

"May every sunrise hold more promise,
and every sunset hold more peace."

~ Unknown

LESSON 10

❧ ❧

*Intuition
and signs*

I AM open to
the signs and
signals that the
universe is
sending me,
I take positive
action in the
light of these.

Lesson 10

Serendipity ~ Signs & Intuition

~ By logic we prove, but by intuition we discover
~ Leonardo Da Vinci

Once you start to align your energy and consciousness with what you want to create, the universe will start to respond to your request and send you signs and signals that will guide you. Before you awakened to your personal and spiritual journey it was probably easy to dismiss these signs as coincidences, but a part of developing and expanding your consciousness is realising that there is actually no such thing!

As you keep your focus on your bigger vision you will find that the masterpiece of your life starts to become like an exercise in painting by numbers. There will be colours and shades that represent life experiences, and twists and turns that you need to paint on the canvas, without knowing at times how these contribute to the overall picture. In your mind's eye though, you know how you want this to turn out, and with every brush stroke you are getting closer. The universe might throw you some additional scenes that you hadn't considered at the outset, and when these come up you may feel that they are spoiling the vision that you are holding dear.

Don't get disheartened, life is often a test of faith, as circumstances, lessons and people all crop up that have some kind of significance or meaning for your greater and higher good. These 'random' occurrences and interactions are actually nothing of the kind, they are the universe signposting you towards what you need to do and experience in order to get what you have asked for. Think of them as cosmic stepping stones! Tuning into *Signs and Intuition* will help you to find why they are all being energetically attracted into your space, and how they are going to contribute overall. For instance it may be your dream and ambition to work in the healing arts and bring lots of support and assistance to many people on their journey, whilst helping yourself to grow and bring income to you as an exchange. Imagine that this is the key message that you are sending out there to the universe and you are focused on this happening in the present moment, affirming and visualising. The universe has heard your request and starts to line up matching frequencies and energies in order to help you to draw in this vision and create your reality, however in order to get to this point in your life there are some other traits that you need to develop. The universe will naturally start to plug any gaps that you need in order to help you behind the scenes, like your own personal assistant.

You may need to meet key people that will help you in terms of premises and training, you may need a life lesson in managing finances or ego, or you may need to experience and overcome a life challenge yourself in order to be authentic and help others. You may not realise in your conscious mind that you need these parts of the puzzle. You need to appreciate and know that if you are aligned to the outcome that you want to manifest, the universe may have to give you some key ingredients that you don't know you are missing. Working with *Signs and*

Intuition will be hugely helpful. Signposts may seem like random events or interactions initially, look for a strong gut feeling associated with the 'random' things coming up more than once. When these things happen there is a will be some kind of relevance to you, and three times especially is a universal nudge to sit up and take notice! Your intuition will give you a strong feeling of knowing that something has been put in your path for a reason, don't let your mind and ego talk you out of this, go where your instincts take you and see how this unfolds.

Intuition is a type of resonance, it's like a connection deep within you, a knowing that points you in the right direction, and there is no way that it can be explained or justified. When I look back at my life, there are times that I did not follow my intuition and usually regretted it, which in itself brought more lessons. Work with *Signs and Intuition* and take these as your calling to take positive action in the direction that you are being shown.

What are the repeating signs and signals that the universe has shown you?

What is the underlying message in these signs?

What action do you need to take as a result of these signs?

"I AM open to the signs and signals that the universe is sending me, I take positive action in the light of these."

LESSON 11

Self love and
loving others

I AM lovable, I love myself and my life experience reflects this back to me in every moment.

Lesson 11

Two Hearts ~ Love Yourself

~ To love oneself is the beginning of a lifelong romance ~ Oscar Wilde

Loving yourself is something that we know we should be doing, but how many of us actually put verbs into the practice of loving ourselves? And what does it really matter anyway?

Learning to *Love Yourself* is *hugely* important. It is really is the cornerstone of your life coming together and your circumstances and relationships blossoming. It's not arrogant or selfish to love who you are, it's necessary. Without this you cannot hope to manifest the life or relationships of your dreams. When you *Love Yourself* you are sending out a vibrational message to the universe saying, "I AM worthy of all things good" and as we have learned thus far, the universe will respond to this and send you whatever version of all things good you are manifesting and focused on, *You Attract What You Are.*

In direct contrast, when you are in an energy of not loving yourself, this sends out the opposite message of "I AM not worthy of anything good" and will create resistance to positive energy and act as a magnet to the negative. Do not confuse this with ego, people that do truly love themselves have often walked a long and challenging journey to get to this point in their lives. To *Love Yourself* means accepting who you are, forgiving yourself, speaking to yourself in kind and encouraging ways, looking after your body, having healthy boundaries and knowing that you are doing your best in every moment. It's about being at peace with *you* in all ways, including past, present and future versions of who you are. Loving yourself is being able to let go of other people's opinions of you and know that this does not affect the way you feel about you.

Our personal and intimate relationships are great testimonies to how we feel about ourselves. When we are prepared to step out of them and observe the patterns that we have attracted, they can be very illuminating about where we are at as individuals. Look at the experiences that you have drawn to you, and they will show you where you are resonating in terms of your own self-love. I know from my past experience that living in an energy of 'not feeling good enough' will be matched up by the universe perfectly to people and situations that give you a whole lot more of not feeling good enough. Years ago, I allowed the tiny reserve of self-worth that I had left to be ripped away from me and trampled on, and I hardly objected at all because after all 'I am not worthy of love' was playing on a loop in my mind and energy field. When I was in a place of not loving myself I drew in people that didn't love me either, and the more I blamed myself for things going bad, the more I attracted criticism from others and believed that I was the cause. For me this was a situation that lasted far too long, and so chronically low was my own self-love that I actually had to be pushed out of the situation kicking and screaming. The way that I thought about myself had stopped me from believing that I was worthy of anything other than what I had, and what I had was certainly not good.

It wasn't until I started to awaken to my spiritual journey and expand my consciousness that I could start to heal and release destructive patterns that I'd held on to for so long. I started to work on loving me and this was the moment that my life started to change in positive ways. I began to see the correlation between how I thought and felt about myself, and what the universe was sending me in my experience.

It was at this time in my life that I was blessed with finding someone that loved me for who I was, interestingly he had been there all along in my social circle, but we had never connected. This could be seen as irony, but I believe that there was an element of divine timing here as well as resonance. Until I had started to release some of my own baggage and start to align my vibration with knowing that I was loveable and deserving, there was no way that the universe could have matched me up with the wonderful man that was waiting all along. Until I had begun to love me I would never have attracted someone that really loved me back, because the vibration was not there to draw it in.

Sometimes as we change, the people that we are close to will also change in resonance and stay aligned with us, in this case relationships will remain in your life and grow. An example of this may be when you go through a lesson with a close friend, family member or partner that you both learn from and both understand in order to shift your consciousness.

My husband and I have shared lessons in compassion and forgiveness in this way, where a third party has wronged us and we have had the opportunity to act in ways to either seek revenge and deliberately damage them, or to act from a higher self-perspective and see the silver lining of the learning we could experience. In this case we talked it through and expressed our feelings, until we came to the conclusion that we would be damaging ourselves by deliberately damaging others.

(This would have been in several ways, we were not at this point experiencing forgiveness and therefore we were carrying around a victim status which was causing resistance to our flow, and also through *Law of Attraction* and *The Law of Karma* wishing negative experiences for others will bring them back to you.)

We both learned the same lesson at the same time and therefore our resonance changed together, and this was a blessing. If one of us had been hell-bent on seeking revenge and the other had wanted to forgive, this would have contributed to a feeling of being on a totally different page from each other. When there is a lot of dissonance in a relationship this can lead to real life discord and arguments as well as a drifting apart of the people involved.

As you change yourself and grow you may reflect back ideas and experiences to people in your life that embrace them and applaud your personal and spiritual development, these people are still in resonance with you. Equally though there could well be people that don't like the new version of you that is more self-empowered and learning to *Love Yourself*, if they are not in this place in themselves. This will be an uncomfortable reflection for them and they will no longer feel in resonance with you. They may make derogatory comments about you changing, try to look past these and know that this is their resistance and not yours.

It's a big part of loving yourself to be able to release yourself from situations that are not in resonance with who you are becoming. Especially if you are afraid of change or a people pleaser, then it's often easier to move your own needs and beliefs further down the list and try to remain the older version of yourself in order to keep the peace. This is self-destructive and will start again to resonate to "I AM not worthy" and you will draw in more of this kind of energy, plus it's exhausting to have to portray yourself as someone that you are not.

You need to draw on as much self-love as you can and know that you are totally worthy of being the person that you are becoming, and that by embracing this you are putting yourself first and this alone is an a sending a vibration to the universe that you *Love Yourself.*

What do you say to yourself that is unkind and unloving?

What is showing up in your life experience as a result?

How can you start to show yourself more love?

"I AM lovable, I love myself and my life experience reflects this back to me in every moment."

LESSON 12

Allow the flow

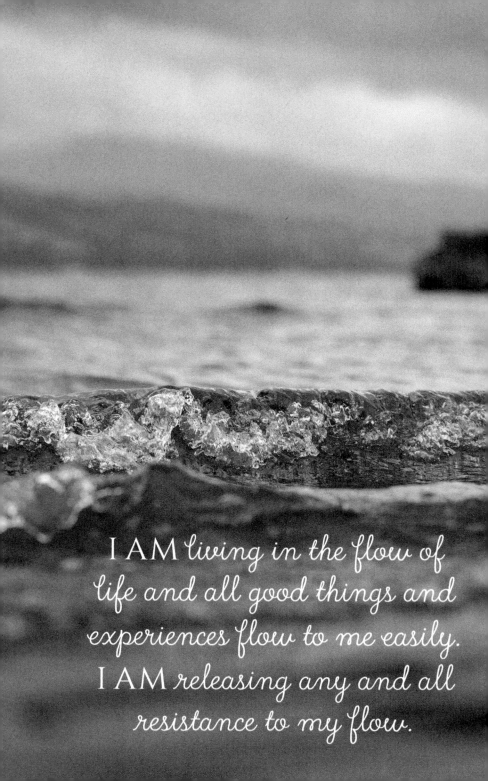

I AM living in the flow of life and all good things and experiences flow to me easily. I AM releasing any and all resistance to my flow.

Lesson 12

The Flow ~ Release Resistance and Allow the Flow of Goodness

~ We must be willing to let go of the life we have planned, so as to have the life that is waiting for us ~ Joseph Campbell

There is a flow that exists in life where all things good are available to us in any moment. This flow is the universal energy all around us, that we can align with and create the life and experiences we desire. Now you have learned about conscious creation and attraction, you can choose to go with the flow of life, or to go against it.

When we are in the flow of life this shows up as things going well for us, being at ease, feeling joy and abundance and having what we need in the moment.

The flow attracts wellness, as things and experiences that you desire seem to come to you easily and with little effort. There is an acceptance that all is well and life is good, with more goodness coming.

People in the flow surrender to life and know that life is occurring as it should be, all that comes their way is in perfect time and for their greatest and highest good. When we are not in the flow the opposite experience is created.

Things don't go our way we feel out of synch, good fortune and opportunity disappear. Obstacles, challenges and other symptoms of disease manifest in our life, relationships and body. Lack of flow makes you feels stuck and the more stuck you feel, the more stuck you are.

It's likely you will have experienced both being in the flow and not, at different times in your life, and we all know which one we would rather have more of.

How can we *Allow the Flow of Goodness* more? Lack of flow is created by resistance. This is a type of *Self-Sabotage* that creates a blockage in the wellbeing and joy that is always there waiting for us to allow it in. Resistance is usually rooted in fear of some description, and this can take many different forms. Imagine resistance and fear as a blockage in the middle of a river that is slowing down the water. This is how we slow down or stop positive energy flowing into our lives. Each blockage in our flow will represent a fear in some aspect of our life and consciousness. Once you have identified what this fear represents you can use different techniques to help break it down and release resistance.

Think for a moment about your own life and an area where things could be better. This could be anything from relationships, health, finances and beyond. Now take a conscious step back from the situation and look at it from a perspective of your own thoughts and where you could be creating resistance. Where are you in fear? And what are you saying to yourself about this situation? Often we create stories and beliefs that may not even be true, these could be inherited from others or created through past experiences and carried over to the now time where they are irrelevant. You know now that thoughts are vibrational and they attract like for like frequencies, and therefore experiences. Can you see where you are creating resistance in this situation and how your thoughts, feelings and consciousness have created blockages in your flow?

Perhaps there is so much fear and resistance that a damn has been built across your flow, and stopped goodness coming in for you altogether?

When you are going through this process try to be mindful of all of the other lessons that you have studied throughout *Twelve Lessons*, and know that if your mind starts to blame other people that these people could be offering you important insights through *The Law of Reflection*, and that *You Cannot Fix Other People*, only yourself. And know that since *You Attract What You* Are then you are in control of changing this. If you truly want to open up your flow to all things good then you will need to take responsibility for your own *Self-Sabotage*, and work on releasing this to allow more goodness to come into your life.

No one of course creates lack of flow or blocks their own opportunities deliberately, so please do not go into a pattern of thinking that anything bad or unfortunate that has ever happened in your life is 'your fault'. This will create more self-sabotage and will become *Old Stuff* that will *Keep You Stuck*. There is more going on in the universe than we know about as humans and you may have experienced some *Cause and Effect*, soul lessons or pre-arranged situations to help you to grow and expand. Beating yourself up does not serve you or anyone else and will send out an 'I'm not worthy' message to the universe and engage your victim mode.

I am a great believer that when we know better, we do better, and part of this is thinking better. You are now armed with knowledge and understanding that you may not have been before and this means that you can now think and behave differently and get different results.

Signs and Intuition are great friends that will help you to stay in the flow. When you intuitively feel that something or someone is not right for you, this is your own inner guidance showing you that there is resistance coming up, and that you will be out of the flow if you go ahead. Learn to honour your feelings and know that when you are in the flow you feel good and when you get out of the flow you feel less than good. Strive to follow your bliss and the feelings of happiness, love and joy whenever you can and this will keep you in alignment with your flow.

Embrace reflections from others about flow and resistance, and know that these are showing you where you where you can improve. Also be aware of your physical body, as aches, pains and symptoms are closely linked to emotional and behavioural patterns of fear and resistance that stop your flow.

Many examples are self-explanatory such as issues with your shoulders representing the feeling that you are carrying huge burdens and responsibilities in your life, and issues with ankles representing a resistance in moving forwards, and embracing the twists and turns of life's journey. For more information and insights into how your body is speaking to you about your flow I highly again recommend the work of *Louise Hay* and her book *You Can Heal Your Life*. Once you know where you are stuck you can use powerful affirmations or seek healing modalities to help you to release the resistance and fear that is holding you back.

The flow is also related to the giving and receiving of energy, and when you are not experiencing this in equal proportion you can find that you cut off your flow. Adopt the attitude that you are living your life with the principle of *fair exchange* and that when you give so shall you receive and vice versa. This is especially good at opening up your financial flow and helping money to move freely in both directions, in and out of your pocket or bank account. Relationships can also be enhanced greatly by the principle of *fair exchange* and deliberately holding this as your intention when you are relating to others can help to release all kinds of resistance and challenge.

Being in the present moment can help you to be in the flow of life. Worrying about the future or raking over and over the past will activate feelings, thoughts and vibrations that could move you out of alignment with the flow that is all around you in the now time, especially if those thoughts and feelings are rooted in low vibration energies such as worry or regret. Become an observer of your own mind and know that when you are drifting in your attention into the past or future, that this is unhelpful and gently bring yourself back to the present moment.

An attitude of gratitude can keep you in the energy of flow, as being grateful for what you have will help you to allow more of what you want to be attracted into your life. Always look for the silver lining in any situation or lesson that you are being faced with. No matter what is going on there will always be something to be in gratitude for and by giving thanks to the universe, *Release Resistance and Allow the Flow of Goodness,* you totally deserve this in your life.

Where is my life not flowing right now?

What is the fear that is creating the resistance in my flow?

What can I do to release this fear and allow more goodness to flow to me?

"I AM living in the flow of life and all good things and experiences flow to me easily. I AM releasing any and all resistance to my flow."

LESSON 13

❧ ❧

Life and
soul lessons

I AM grateful for all of
my lessons and the gifts
that they bring me for
my growth and evolution
as a soul on earth.

Lesson 13

Lessons ~ Life and Soul Lessons

~ Some people come in our life as blessings, some people come in as lessons ~Mother Teresa

We all come to earth with a unique soul curriculum full of lessons that are specific to us. If we avoid learning these lessons, life will often turn up the volume and bring them back around. This is why so many of us seem to attract a different version of the same situation time and time again – we have not learned what we were supposed to in order to help us.

This can be frustrating, but getting frustrated will only create resistance and block your learning even more. Try to stand back, get centred and look at the situation from a higher-self perspective. Ask yourself what you are missing here. What do you need to learn or to heal in order to change your vibration?

Trust in your intuition and the signs and signals that the universe is sending you in order to help you understand and navigate your way through this. It is also important to know that just as we have our own soul curriculum, so do others. This means that they are experiencing situations in their lives that are great learning opportunities, specific to them. The kind-hearted person that you are may want to charge in and rescue them when a lesson unleashes its heartache and struggle on another, especially if it is someone you love.

I'm not going to say don't help, but I am going to say that it is important not to rescue. Allow them the learning that they need from the situation, and if a full-on rescue is unavoidable, then perhaps their lesson is wrapped up in gratitude, humility, faith in humanity or taking responsibility. Always know that each one of us is here to experience, learn and grow as a soul, and never rob someone of that opportunity, no matter how well-meaning you are. Hold an intention that you are empowering both of you.

I believe that when we set foot on our spiritual path, we start to send a vibration out to the universe that we want to learn, heal, grow and expand. The universe hears this as your overall intention and starts to help you out. Think about it in terms of Law of Attraction – your outcome is to be more enlightened and healed as a soul, and in order to get there to that ultimate goal with which you are aligned, the universe needs to start joining up some dots. You need to experience some more earthly lessons in order to evolve, and by walking a more spiritual path in life, you can find that lessons are accelerated to help you to make progress faster.

The thing is that very often lessons don't feel like the gift they truly are. Little lessons come along on a daily basis, our patience is tried and life throws us the odd curve ball. But what about the big stuff?

Life lessons can be wrapped up in struggle and pain, they can make you feel like you are drowning in a sea of overwhelm and desperation. They can whip up such a storm in your life that you feel wholly battle-scarred and mangled beyond belief.

Life Lessons change us on many levels, but the change really comes from the processing, the healing and the personal journey that each experience offers you. We have the choice to come out of the storm a different person, and although our exterior may be as fragile as spun sugar, the fire we have walked through has forged a strength deep inside of us that is evident in time.

Each lesson brings a gift, and the greater the lesson the bigger that gift. Keep this as your focus when you face something really challenging, and know that even when you can't see it, the gift will appear in time.

Start seeing your challenges on earth as lessons, and find it in your heart to be grateful for them, or at least hold the intention that one day you will be able to. Notice when lessons come up, and work hard to stay out of the drama that so many of them can create. Step back, and ask for the essence of the lesson, why it is playing out at this time and what it is teaching you. Go deep within yourself and be honest about your human moments and what you can improve on, how is life supporting and guiding you towards a better version of yourself?

Remember that when you are sharing a lesson with another person that they could be gaining something different to you through the process – the same lesson, but a different experience and gift for them. Honour both of you as best you can and know that this soul has stepped forwards to help you at this time, and you have to help them, even if it feels that this is not the case.

What life lessons have I experienced so far?

What was the gift in these lessons?

How will these lessons help me to move forward?

"I AM grateful for all of my lessons and the gifts that they bring me for my growth and evolution as a soul on earth."

LESSON 14

Be here now

I AM present, fully connected to myself and the earth and enjoying every moment as it unfolds in the here and now.

Lesson 14

The Present ~ Be Here Now

~ For the present is the point at which time touches eternity ~ CS Lewis

Being present in the moment is all about bringing your consciousness into the now time entirely. It is about stilling the incessant habit we have as personalities, egos and minds that drives us to think about things constantly. We rake over what has occurred in the past and we worry about what is going to happen in the future, but we are rarely in the now.

As humans we gather up all of our experiences throughout our lives and we use them as a framework or a map of reality (our own reality, not actual reality) to help us make sense of the world and give things context. This means that we are always comparing people and circumstances to what has occurred in our past, or other reference points like cultural beliefs, mind viruses or what someone once told us to be true.

Being present means doing what you can to stop looking through that filter. When you are able to be fully in the now, you are able to perceive life in a different way that is not as limiting and can be far more fulfilling. You don't judge things or people as wrong or right, you are more accepting and you have more inner peace, stillness and joy. You appreciate more and you are in gratitude more, you don't hound yourself with expectations and wrack yourself with regret.

Being mindful and living consciously will help you. Observing your own mind and knowing that this is a facet of you, but not who you actually are, is useful. Noticing when you are not present (and for many of us this is most of the time) and then gently steering your consciousness back into the moment is the key.

Life can take on a new simplicity.

And in terms of Law of Attraction, being present is key.

You need to activate the feeling that what you want is happening now, and by now, I mean in the present. This is what the universe matches and then sends you an experience that you desire.

Magic happens in the moment, do what you can to show up.

What can I do to become more present?

Am I avoiding being present because I am struggling with something?

When do I tend to be least present and how can I change this?

"I AM present, fully connected to myself and the earth and enjoying every moment as it unfolds in the here and now."

"Someone once said I was deluded,
I nearly fell off my unicorn."

~ Unknown

LESSON 15

❦

Discernment

I AM safe and free to exercise the power of choice over all parts of my life. I honour and respect myself by having discernment. I spend my precious time and energy with people and in situations that are in alignment with my greater good and who I AM.

Lesson 15

Empowered Choices ~ Discernment

~ You cannot change the people around you, but you can choose the people that you choose to be around ~ Unknown

Discernment simply means the power to choose. Different people and situations come into our experience of life, and some feel like they are a good fit whilst others don't. Your intuition is your greatest ally when it comes to exercising discernment, it will work hard to give you a heads up on what will serve you and what won't. You might get a niggling doubt or a full on pom-pom parade as it tries to alert you to the fact that there is an energy mis-match going on, that you are not in alignment with a person or situation, and that this is not going to be a great move or alliance for you.

Tuning into that feeling is the beginning of being able to exercise discernment, and the second step is taking action and either creating distance and boundaries, or a complete separation. In between, of course, are all the feelings of guilt and obligation and human moments where you wrestle with yourself. Your intuition is telling you that you really need to stop hanging around with a group of friends, or that you should look for another job, or that you should avoid someone altogether because their drama has become a drain.

There is a part of you that knows you need to protect your own energy and have better boundaries, but it feels rather mean to actually start the process. This is especially hard if you have previously been close to someone, and because of your own inner work and growth, you have lifted your vibration and you now feel a dissonance in the energy of that relationship. Perhaps there is some healing to be done between you that will bridge the gap? Maybe some honesty about who you are becoming as a person and how they might fit into your life in a different way?

The more you change and evolve, the smaller your circle may get. That's because so many people are not yet awake to the divine multidimensional being that they are, and they are playing small and stuck in earthly drama. That is not said with any judgement, it's simply an observation. People wake up when it's right for them, but when you are awake, unconscious relationships can be very hard work.

So what can you do about it?

Set an intention that you are acting with grace and ease and invite these universal principles into your life. Also know that if the energy does not feel right from your point of view then it won't be right for them either, but they may not see this. Allow yourself to create better boundaries with people and situations that you no longer feel in alignment with. Look to take positive action where you can in order to help yourself and honour your own feelings. Cut cords with people and situations that drain you after any and all contact, this includes thoughts that you have about them. This will help to create distance and keep your energy clear. Make sure you do this with a loving intention for all concerned.

And the final and possibly most important observation is to be really selective about who and what you give your energy and attention to as you move forward in your life. Don't hang around in Facebook groups that are negative and full of whingers, don't heavily associate with people that are committed to their drama, don't watch violent movies or put yourself in chaotic and negative energy.

Check in with your gut, see how you feel and then act as best you can in a way that honours that.

How can I support myself to make better choices of where I spend my time and energy and with whom?

What am I doing in my life right now that I can change and exercise discernment in?

Where do I need better boundaries in my life or relationships?

"I AM safe and free to exercise the power of choice over all parts of my life. I honour and respect myself by having discernment. I spend my precious time and energy with people and in situations that are in alignment with my greater good and who I AM."

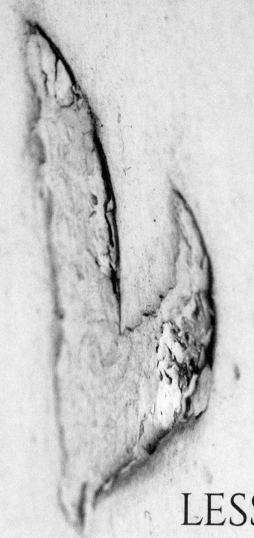

LESSON 16

~⚬~

*Heal your
wounds*

I AM healing
from my past
because I deserve
to feel good in
my present.

Lesson 16

Healing ~ Heal Your Wounds

~ Although the world is full of suffering, it is full also of overcoming it ~ Helen Keller

Part of the human condition is the fact that throughout our lifetime, shit happens. We end up having to go through situations and experiences that are challenging in so many different ways, ranging from moments of sadness right through to times that are absolutely harrowing. That's life folks, and I can't pixie and unicorn it up for you. Of course we have an intention that things are going well for us, and we know that in every moment of struggle there is somewhere a gift, but that dissolves when you are in the thick of it and something is happening that derails you.

I have been through some very big stuff (according to me!) Everyone perceives their stuff as being big stuff, don't they? Depending on when it hits and how you are feeling, you may or may not have depleted resilience and something could feel bigger than it actually is. If you feel overwhelmed, then a good question to ask is "What's the worst thing that could happen here?" Very often this will give you some perspective to be able to see that actually it's not as bad as you first thought.

Time is a healer, but when life has kicked the shiz out of you sometimes time alone doesn't cut it. Depending on the experience and the wound that it's left in your heart and soul, you may be able to heal it with time and forgiveness, or you may not.

The important thing to know here is that if you can heal it you would feel so much better and you would attract a lot more goodness in your life. Old stuff that happened to you years ago can still have an incredible hold if you haven't processed and released it yet, and every now and then someone will say something or a song will come on the radio, or you'll get a universal red flag to show you that this still bothers you. If it bothers you, then it's a wound that needs healing.

Now for some of you reading this you may be thinking, "what does she know, she has no idea how my ex-husband cheated and left me high and dry with debts and kids and heartbreak…" or something similar that relates to your story.

I admit it, I have no idea what you have been through.

BUT I know that is your ego talking, defending its drama and refusing to let you move forward.

You are worthy of healing your past. And just in case you feel like you need permission – I'm giving you it, right here, right now. Start getting really honest with yourself. Ask yourself what you are carrying around that is unresolved. What chapters in your history still bring you sadness, unworthiness and pain when you look back? What do you need to move on from and stop beating yourself or others up about? What do you need to resolve so that you can have peace of mind and joy in the moment?

You'll know what it is, and when you have named it you need to make a personal commitment that you are going to work on it and help yourself to heal. When I have stuff like this going on I get help. If something in my life has proven to be bigger than me and I can't shift it on my own and time is ticking by, I reach out. That's not weak, that's smart.

"But I can't afford it," is a common objection from the ego at this point.

Can you seriously afford not to? This stuff is blocking your flow and pinching off the joy and happiness you could be wallowing in. You are worthy of healing, I promise you, and this process will not only help you but other people in your life as well as you can be more present and have a more authentic connection.

And if you really can't afford to get some help then look for someone that will give you a discount or trade a skill that you have with them, holding the intention for a fair exchange and the right person coming along to help you at the perfect time.

What old wounds am I carrying that need to be healed?

Why have I been afraid of taking this healing journey?

What can I do to help myself heal these wounds?

"I AM healing from my past because I deserve to feel good in my present."

LESSON 17

Ditch the drama

I AM living a peaceful life that is full of joy, abundance, love and happiness.

Lesson 17

Drama Queen ~ Ditch the Drama

~ Pour yourself a drink, put on some lipstick and pull yourself together ~ Liz Taylor

Drama is a drain on your time and energy. It keeps you stuck in the same story, and therefore the same energy vibration that created your trauma, upset or issue in the first place is still playing out. This means you cannot move on in a literal sense, and in an energetic sense it means that you will draw more of the same kind of situation in.

Our ego loves a bit of drama, and so does our inner victim. They love it so much that they will often try to recruit other people into the drama that we have created by gossiping, posting things on social media, texting and talking about the drama. If someone is stuck in the drama and really entrenched in it, they will not want to leave. It has become their story and they will not be happy if you try to coax them out of it.

You will see their resistance when you offer them suggestions of what they could do in order to change or improve their circumstances. They will tell you straight up why that won't work, usually without considering any positive input. This is the ego defending itself and wanting to remain in the drama. You can try to change the subject that you are talking about, but either immediately or ultimately the conversation will be steered towards poor them and their drama.

The reason that people usually want to stay in their drama is that there is some kind of payoff for them. This payoff could be that people give them sympathy, or maybe that not too much is expected from them because they are seen as wounded or fragile. There are many different payoffs that someone could be gaining for being stuck, but it's important to know that people usually cannot see this. If they are not awake to living a conscious life, then they may be completely unaware of their drama, and they may be receiving the payoff on a subconscious level. When you know better, you do better, and maybe they have not gained enough life experience or self-awareness yet to see that things could be different – have compassion but do not get sucked in!

(If this is sounding like you, then it's great that you have identified that you might be stuck. I think we all have a secret drama queen archetype that loves to come out and play. But being mindful of that and knowing when we go into that energy, is the first step towards staying out of the drama.)

The best way to deal with it is to have good boundaries with this type of person, make sure that you give yourself a way out or exit route when it comes to spending time with them before they (unintentionally) suck all of your energy away. Don't allow yourself to be available all of the time. Yes if it's a matter of life or death, then of course you will step up and help. But if their drama plays out on a Saturday night after a bottle of wine and yet another argument with him indoors, then you may want to respond to the text messages the following day and do a breezy check-in to see that they are ok, rather than spending two hours of your life playing drunken text tag. Make sure also that you have an intention that your life is a drama-free zone, and work hard to notice when you tend to create your own drama – then get out of it fast. Remember that you attract what you are, and therefore when you are the kind of person that is less likely to have drama going on in their own life, you will attract people that are less likely too. If you feel drama creeping up then be aware of it and change your focus and your self-talk. Remind yourself that this does not serve you and it will keep you stuck, and you are worth more than that.

Use some basic protection and cord cutting techniques with people in your life regularly in order to keep your energy clear, and especially with people that are energy drains in your life because of their tendency towards drama.

Where in my life am I being sucked into my own drama or other people's?

What is the perceived payoff for this?

How can I help myself to ditch the drama in my life?

"I AM living a peaceful life that is full of joy, abundance, love and happiness."

LESSON 18

❧

Put down
what is heavy

I AM releasing
my own burdens
and the need to
carry others
for them.

Lesson 18

Burdens ~ Put Down What is Heavy

~ Let go or be dragged ~ Zen Proverb

The shit cart is a great metaphor for the stuff that we drag around with us that we need to process and dump! This lesson is an expansion of Heal Your Wounds. Carrying old unprocessed issues wears us out. It drains our energy and means that we cannot be fully present in the moment. There is always the danger of someone mentioning something that shines a search light on a part of you that is still trapped in fear, or resentment or unworthiness from the past. This can make us feel exposed and vulnerable all over again, because the original wound is not healed and we are still carrying around all of the emotional baggage connected to the past trauma.

There are all kinds of reasons that we as humans do this.

It's painful to go through our old stuff. As we evolve however, and become more conscious, we see that it's far more painful to carry this hurt for a lifetime, than to go through the comparatively short term process of healing. There are different ways to heal and let go of the burdens that weigh you down, and not all of them involve you ending up feeling completely mangled. When I went through some big, big stuff in my life I found that energy therapies really helped me. I did have a brief course of counselling which helped me to identify the issues that were playing out, and once I had recognized what I needed to work on I didn't need to keep talking about it. Although I didn't know it at the time, this would have kept the story active in my vibration and stopped me from making progress, so my inner drama queen reluctantly hung up her tiara. Do what you need to in order to see what you are dragging around that is not serving you, then once you know, give yourself the gift of setting yourself free, however that looks to you.

A note on other people's shit carts - I know so many people that have a habit of seeing someone struggling with their overloaded stuff, that run in and help them. This turns into them dragging two carts up the hill called life and they end up exhausted, and resentful because the other person won't sort their shit out! The irony is that they haven't had a chance to because you are so busy taking over and "helping". Don't get me wrong I know this came from a good place initially.

Remember that you can't fix other people, you need to support them to fix themselves. Pump up the wheels on their shit cart and give them a torch so they can have a proper good look at what they are carrying, then get about your own business of healing.

What are you dragging around that you need to release?

Are you dragging someone else's cart as well as your own?

What excuses are you making about not moving on?

"I AM releasing my own burdens and the need to carry others' for them."

"Be happy with what you have, while working for what you want."

~ Helen Keller

LESSON 19

⚜

Protect yourself

I AM setting myself free from any and all negative influences, caused by me and others. I know everyone is doing their version of their best and I release us all with love and light.

Lesson 19

Psychic Attack ~ Protect Yourself

*~ Fools take a knife and stab people in the back.
The wise take a knife, cut the cord and free
themselves from the fools ~ Unknown*

Everything is energy, and that includes our thoughts and intentions. Sometimes in life we meet people that tick us off, upset us or piss on our parade like a tsunami. Our human reaction is to think of them in a less than awesome way, and maybe even wish them (what we perceive to be) their karma in all its glory, preferably with a front row seat reserved for us. We think about them in spiteful ways and wish that life would send them a shit storm, maybe like the one they created for us.

Yes it's spiritual to forgive, but you can do that later, after the seething. And your ego just loves that view from the moral high ground, being right is great... isn't it? They shat on you so they deserve your contempt, end of. The thing is though, you are not only sending thoughts and feelings their way, you are sending energy. This is relevant in two ways, firstly you are creating a lower vibration negative energy cord their way and perpetuating your inner victim's party. Secondly, you know that Law of Attraction sends you back what you give out... do you want someone sending you a whole load of nasty because you messed up? There are two ways to look at psychic attack, you doing it to others and you being on the receiving end. Firstly, if you are the one that is creating it, you probably have not done it on purpose so lighten up on yourself. Secondly, know that this does not serve you. By focusing thoughts and energy in their direction that are of a negative nature, you are staying stuck in a situation that you feel bad about. You are actually harming yourself and not them, so do what you can to move on and release.

Some ideas include writing a heartfelt letter to them and burning it with the intention of clearing the energy between you, asking that cords are cut or putting them into your freezer. The freezer technique is a great way of freezing their influence out of your life both metaphorically and literally as you write someone's name on a piece of paper and draw around it with a pen. A yellow pen is the best symbolically but really it doesn't matter too much, your intention overrides everything else. Speaking of which, it's super important that you hold an intention that you are freezing the influence out of this situation on your own life, and that you wish everyone the best possible outcome.

Don't do this if you cannot generate that feeling or at least get close. Never do anything like this whilst deliberately wishing harm on someone. Now place one hand on your heart chakra and the other over their name and do your best to open your heart. Say "I bind you with light" three times, then fold and place in a small plastic bag or container, fill with water and freeze. I still have someone between the fish fingers and bread buns from last year that I froze for a friend. But what if the situation is reversed?

You know you have royally peed someone off and they are wishing all kinds of harm on you. They may not know about energy, but that doesn't matter, their thoughts and intentions are enough to drag you down in all kinds of ways. When you are under psychic attack you can feel really out of balance.

Common symptoms include:
- Nightmares
- Tired and depleted of energy
- Feeling watched
- Unexplained anxiety
- Feeling overwhelmed and emotional
- Inability to concentrate
- Unexplained physical or emotional symptoms

(You must take responsibility for yourself and seek medical guidance if you need to.) You can literally feel someone sending you a bad vibe, especially if you are energy sensitive. So what can you do about it? Firstly, don't go into fear about it, fear lowers your vibration and will attract in more horrible energy you don't want. Remember that before you read this you had probably ticked off loads of people in your lifetime and survived to tell the tale.

Secondly, try to shift your focus and not send the situation or the person in question any energy, this will create more cords between you. Thirdly, cut cords between you. More of that in the woo-woo section.

You may also want to ramp up your energetic protection, but make sure that you do this from a place of wanting to keep your vibration high and reflect anything back to other parties with love and light. It is easy to think of protection as something you need because you are being attacked, and that is not a vibration that you want to perpetuate and draw in more of a match.

Which people in my life from my past or present may have sent me energy that is affecting me in a negative way?

What can I do about this, being mindful that I don't want to attract more by wishing them harm?

Who have I wished harm on in the past or present that I need to cut cords with and wish well for now?

"I AM setting myself free from any and all negative influences, caused by me and others. I know everyone is doing their version of their best and I release us all with love and light."

"Drama doesn't just walk into your life.
You create it, invite it or hang out with it."

~ Unknown

LESSON 20

❦

*Love
your body*

I AM *loving my body by making conscious choices that nurture it with goodness.*

Lesson 20

Physical Nurturing ~ Love Your Body

~ Take care of your body, it's the only place you
have to live in ~ Jim Rohn

Our bodies are the house of our soul, and we have a
responsibility to take care of them. Looking after your
body is an act of self-love, and when we don't look after
our bodies it is often due to a deep-rooted feeling of not
being worthy. Think about it for a moment, if we truly
loved ourselves and felt truly worthy then why would we
treat our bodies in a way that we know does not serve us?

Poor food choices, not enough water, depleted sleep and
self-reproaching thoughts, all have an effect on our bodies
and can lead us towards illness. None of us consciously
want to create this for ourselves, so why do we do it?
Because we are human and we are a work in progress, fact
but not excuse. Healing your old wounds and starting to
build up your own self-worth will help you hugely in
looking after your body. Being conscious of the decisions
you make on a day to day basis, stepping back and asking
yourself "does this serve me?" will create a moment in
time and space where you can change habits and make
better choices.

There is so much information out there about what is
good for you and what is not, that it's mind boggling!
Take responsibility and find out what could work for you.
In my experience, when I eat a plant based diet and cut out

meat and dairy, I feel like I have a lot more energy and wellbeing. There is evidence to support that this is a healthy way to eat and can ward off illness, and help as part of a recovery plan if you are suffering from a condition. Empower yourself and exercise due diligence, and once you have worked out what you feel will be good to support your own health and wellbeing, get a plan and get started! Even small improvements such as drinking more water can have massive benefits on the way you feel and function.

The way you think and feel about your body also has an effect on it. Remember that thoughts are energetic, and thoughts that you repeat over and over become affirmations and start to attract in the outcome that you are focussed on. For example telling yourself that you are fat is not ever going to make you lose weight, and telling yourself that you are tired will never give you more energy.

Be conscious about the thoughts that you are sending to your body and make sure that they are thoughts of health, wellbeing and love. Send gratitude to your senses, your organs and your spine, all parts of you that function as a unit in order for you to be here in the physical.

What am I doing that is harming my body?

What could I do to show my body more love?

What are the wounds that are making me feel unworthy of having a healthy and beautiful body and how can I heal them?

"I AM loving my body by making conscious choices that nurture it with goodness."

"Be who you are and say what you feel,
because those who mind don't matter,
and those who matter don't mind."

~ Dr Seuss

LESSON 21

Believe in miracles

I AM easily attracting and experiencing miracles in my life, because I am worthy of them.

Lesson 21

Miracles ~ Believe in Miracles

~ I am realistic, I expect miracles ~

Dr Wayne Dyer

Like anything else in our lives, miracles can only manifest when we believe in them. When we are closed down and adopt an attitude that they aren't real, this creates a vibration in our energy system that is not in any way aligned with the possibility that a miracle could occur. This therefore keeps them firmly at bay for us, and when they don't show up our ego loves nothing better than jumping on the "told you so" bandwagon, which in turn generates more evidence to our human brain that miracles simply do not exist.

This process creates a concrete belief that a miracle is not going to show up in our lives, no matter how badly we might need one. Our beliefs underpin our thoughts and those thoughts are magnetic. When you think this way you are sending out a message to the universe that you are not open for attracting a miracle, so even if they did exist, you certainly aren't going to be taking delivery of one any time soon!

So how can you open up your life to miracles?

You have to start believing that they exist!

And they do, all around us in our everyday lives and in the universe as a whole. You are a living, breathing miracle and so is the whole of creation. Start to look around you and find evidence of miracles so that you can start to get more into alignment with them. Do what you can to step back from your mind and your ego when they whisper to you that miracles aren't real, observe and acknowledge but then start using an affirmation that moves you towards a vibration of knowing that they are.

When you witness a miracle, send energy and focus to it and deliberate gratitude for what you have witnessed. Adopt an expectation that your life is full of miracles and that you experience them every day, this will open you far more to the possibility of attracting them.

Where are you blocking miracles in your life?

How can you bring more miracles into your awareness?

Does part of you feel unworthy of a miracle, and how can you heal this?

"I AM easily attracting and experiencing miracles in my life, because I am worthy of them."

"All you need is faith, trust and
a little pixie dust."

~ Tinkerbell to Peter Pan

LESSON 22

Don't stay a victim

I AM stronger and wiser because of the life lessons I have lived and healed through. Life is always supporting me and I AM loved. I can release the past with peace in my heart.

Lesson 22

Betrayal ~ Don't Stay a Victim

~ Sometimes the person you would take a bullet
for, ends up being the person behind the trigger ~
Taylor Swift

When we experience betrayal in our lives it is a natural
human reaction to go into victim mode. We are likely to
experience emotions such as anger, hatred and a "poor
me" mindset. Depending on what has happened and how
you perceive it, there will be a varying amount of negative
emotion and the amount of time that you hang onto this
part of your story will differ.

I'm not going to say that it's easy to move on from
betrayal, because sometimes it's not, but it is wholly
necessary for your own wellbeing on many levels. Think
of it in terms of Law of Attraction. If you are constantly
feeling wounded you are sending out a vibrational pattern
that says, "I AM a victim of betrayal." The universe will
hear that and respond and you will continue to get
experiences that match this. If you are currently feeling
like you are in victim mode you may have read that last
statement as me "blaming" you for attracting the initial
betrayal. Just so you know, I'm not, that's your ego
kicking in. So someone shat on you monumentally, where
do you go from here? The best way for you to set yourself
free from the negative feelings and emotions of betrayal is
to dig really deep and find a way to have compassion for

the person involved and start to send them love. If your betrayal is recent or you are very entrenched in the drama of it, you're not going to like this idea one bit. You are going to feel that they are not worthy of compassion of love, and that they took something from you (money, a lover, self-worth).

Stop and step back from the drama of the situation and how you feel right now. Ask yourself why they did what they did, and don't allow your ego to take over. Were they feeling financially desperate? Had they fallen in love with someone else and couldn't face telling you? Had they spun a web of lies that meant there was no going back until it was too late? Their behaviour will have been motivated by something that felt uncomfortable and it is likely that they could well be living with remorse and guilt as a result, even if you don't see this.

What has happened, has happened. There is nothing you can do about it now, but you can change the way you look at it. There are two universal laws that might help you here, one is The Law of Attraction and the other is The Law of Divine Compensation. The Law of Attraction is relevant in two ways. Firstly, you don't want to attract a load of stuff you don't want because you are in victim mode, someone shat on you in the past so don't let them shit on your present. Secondly, whatever anyone sends out, they are going to receive a version of that back at some point. The universe has it covered, you don't need to be the cosmic police. Know that what's right for us will be attracted in and that they have some stuff coming their way that is in alignment with who they are. Make sure however that you do not fall into the trap of wishing bad karma on them, you don't want that to come back to you. Do what you can to release and let it go, and wish them well.

Wish them well? You must be kidding. Do you know how hard that would be? And living with all of the hatred and pain and negative emotion is easy is it? You're doing this for you not them, so get your ego out of it and give yourself a chance here. Fake it 'til you make it, sunshine. Remember lesson 1? At least be open to the possibility that you can do this and start moving towards setting yourself free. You may not have heard of The Law of Divine Compensation, but it's certainly worth a mention here. This is a universal law that states that when something is taken from you, it's not taken at all (and believing so will put you in an energy of lack and block your flow). Everything that you need to flourish is held by the universe in the etheric for you, and if you can move on from the experience of betrayal and know that what's right for you can still come in for you, open your heart and align with your greatest good, then you can draw in bigger and better than you think you had. Send them love and send them off, you don't need to carry this anymore. And just in case you are wondering, the worst kind of betrayal is when you betray yourself. Be true to who you are, you are worthy of being here and being loved simply for being your own precious self.

Where in my life might I be stuck in a victim mindset?

What do I need to do to move out of feeling like a victim?

Who or what is stopping me from doing this?

"I AM stronger and wiser because of the life lessons I have lived through and healed through. Life is always supporting me and I AM loved. I can release the past with peace in my heart."

LESSON 23

*Walk the path
for you*

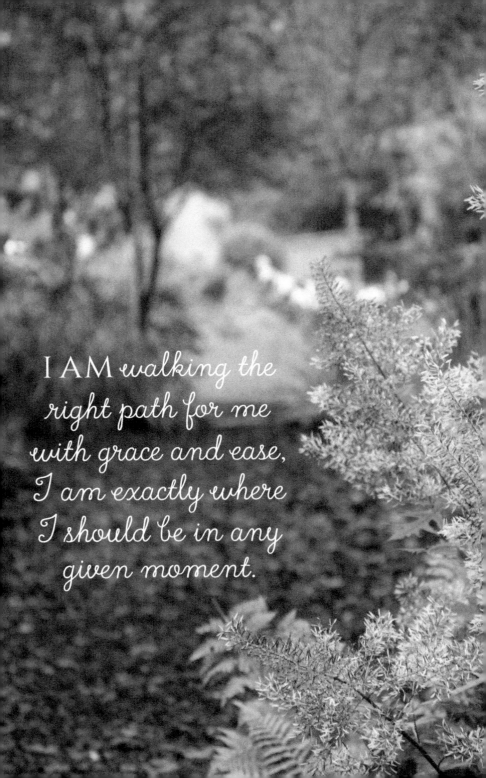

I AM *walking the right path for me with grace and ease, I am exactly where I should be in any given moment.*

Lesson 23

Soul Path ~ Walk the Path for You

~ You are the universe expressing itself as a
human for a little while ~ Eckhart Tolle

You are here as part of the divine plan, no one is here by accident. You are a precious and important soul that is needed here on the earth, with a purpose and a soul path that will help you and others.

The ultimate purpose that we all share as humans is to live in joy and abundance here on the earth. An abundance of health, of love, of wellbeing, of peace of mind and joy. Our soul path is always wanting to take us towards our highest and greatest good, but often we betray and harm ourselves by making choices that do not serve us. When this happens we usually get a warning from our intuition, or we start to feel less in alignment with who we are. We experience negative emotions, a loss of self-worth and a general feeling that we are on the wrong path.

There is no such thing as the wrong path, you are where you are meant to be in every moment. These moments are sent as an opportunity for you to learn and recognize that you have taken a detour somewhere along the way.

If you are experiencing pain and discomfort in your life, it's because you need to change what you are doing, realign and start putting your soul in the driving seat. So many of us stay in relationships, jobs and situations that make us want to shrivel up and die. I know that you may not always have the option to pack up and leave, but at least be honest with yourself and see that this is not what you came here for. It feels bad because it is bad for you, and your discomfort is your resistance to changing that.

When your life path starts to harm you, you have taken a wrong turn. The lessons are likely to come in thick and fast for you in this situation, and you need to go back to your heart and the compass of your soul to find out what you need to change.

When you are walking your path and living your purpose you will find that you are able to spend more time in the flow of life. Things will be easier, opportunities will knock at your door and the dots will start to join up in ways that you didn't expect. Don't confuse your soul path with your occupation, your human work is often not your soul work. Your soul path is going to lead you towards ways that you can heal yourself, live more consciously and be in service. Whatever that looks like in your life, find that and do more of it, this is truly walking your soul path.

How can I align more with my soul path?

What might be preventing me from walking my path?

Is there any part of me that feels unworthy of walking my path, and how can I heal this?

"I AM walking the right path for me with grace and ease, I am exactly where I should be in any given moment."

"You get in life what you have
the courage to ask for."

~ Oprah Winfrey

LESSON 24

Your message to the world

I AM *living my life as a message to the world of who I am in truth.*

Lesson 24

Messenger - Your Message to the World

~ Your life is your message to the world, make sure it's inspiring ~ Unknown

We all have a message that we can share with the world to help others. This may be rooted in a one off moment or experience that you can recall that triggered an epiphany, or it could be years of experience in something. Whatever it is, you have something that you can share with others that will help them on their path. This could be something big or small, profound or whimsical, but it's there.

The message that you have may be yours to impart to people one by one as you interact with them, or it may be something that you demonstrate by the way that you live. It could be the values that you have and the integrity that you have learned that you share with your children, as you raise them to have self-worth and respect others. It may be the tenacity that you have shown in building your own business or picking yourself up after a huge life event. It could be the fact that you know about autistic children, vegan diets, the male menopause, gardening, upcycling furniture, emotional intelligence or being kind to people that have wronged you.

Your message is going to be something positive that you have taken from your life story, something scattered with nuggets of wisdom, encouragement and learning for other people that they can use to enrich their own lives.

You have something to share with the world, one person at a time or en masse, so know that you are valued and needed and find your voice. Whatever that looks like in your life – get it out there!

What can I bring to the world?

How can I share my message with the world?

Is there a part of me that is afraid of sharing my message and how can I heal this?

"I AM living my life as a message to the world of who I am in truth."

Summary of Lessons

Be Open to Possibility
Self-sabotage
You Attract What You Are
Release What Does Not Serve You
You are a Creator
The Law of Karma
The Law of Reflection
Compassion and Forgiveness
You can't fix Other People
Intuition, Signs and Signals
Self-love and Loving Others
Release Resistance & Allow the Flow
Life & Soul Lessons
Be Here Now
Discernment
Heal Your Wounds
Ditch the Drama
Put Down What is Heavy
Protect Yourself
Love your Body
Believe in Miracles
Don't Stay a Victim
Walk the Path for You
Your Message to the World

PRACTICAL
MAGIC

"Those who don't believe in magic will never find it."

Roald Dahl

Cutting Etheric Cords

Etheric Cords are another name for energy cords that bind us to people, places and situations in the present or the past. These cords run energy in one or both directions and can be as thin and wispy as a hair or as thick as a rope.

Cords often keep us tied energetically to people and things that we need to detach from, and they can leave us feeling quite drained. Another effect that cords can have is that you can pick up energy from people and places in your physical body, energy body and emotions. In other words, someone else's stuff can show up for you and you may find that you have their anxiety, their low self-worth or their anger. You can even find that you experience physical symptoms that they have going on, in your own body.

A lot of people think that it's mean to cut cords with people, but in energy terms and done with a loving intention, the process is necessary to keep your own energy clear, and part of working with energy in a responsible way. If you really are worried about being nasty to someone by disconnecting yourself then you can do a general cord cutting with the intention that any cords which do not serve you are removed, and not just them specifically.

I like to cut cords every night before I go to sleep as a matter of course so that I know I am keeping my energy as clear as possible, here's how.

Ask that all parts of you are present, breathe and get in to your heart energy.

Invoke the presence of Archangel Michael, simply by asking him to draw close to you now and support you in cutting cords that do not serve.

Give him permission to work in your aura and use his sword of truth to cut and seal any cords that bind you at this time. You may feel or sense this process, breathe and relax for a few moments and know that this is happening. You may find that you yawn or sigh as the cords are released, or you may feel a sense of freedom or a wave of emotion. Know that all is well and allow the process.

After a few moments give thanks for what you have received and ask Archangel Michael to surround you in protective white light that will help to keep your energy clear and stop new cords from attaching.

You can do this any time of day or night and in any situation, apply it to a board meeting where someone is pulling you down, a divorce where you are held over a financial barrel, or even just your day to day life as you interact with people that might unintentionally cord you.

It is important to know that cords can reattach, so doing this a few times a week is very helpful. They are more likely to attach after an interaction with the person in question, or sometimes even just thinking or speaking about them.

Cutting cords on old situations can help you move forwards from them and heal, and the process can help you to move forward in your life and make progress towards new situations. Cutting cords with a property that you want to sell can be effective when you want to move house, and on past challenges to set you free of their influence.

Daily Protection Ritual

A great way to keep your vibration high and your energy clear is to do a daily ritual. I do mine in the shower every morning, for three reasons – firstly, I can more or less guarantee that I am going to be alone. Secondly, it sets me up for the day, and thirdly, the running water adds a great metaphor to the process.

Here's how it goes.

Releasing any energy that you have picked up that does not serve you is the first part of the process. As the water flows over your body, visualize letting go of anything stuck, anything low in vibration and anything that does not serve you. You may imagine this as etheric cords being dissolved, astral energies, old thought forms and beliefs or general meh that you want to ditch. In your mind's eye see it being washed out of your aura and disappearing down the plug hole.

Next call on the universe to bring you high vibrational love and light, and as the warm water connects with your crown intend that you are a part of the flow. Know that this energy is bringing you protection so that any and all negativity will bounce right off you like you are wearing cosmic Teflon. You will attract loads more awesome and goodness and you'll be loving the joy, happiness and abundance that the day has in store. This is a good time to thank the universe in advance for all the good stuff that is being delivered today, and get into a feeling of thankful anticipation for the day ahead.

Moon Cycle Magic

The energy of the moon affects us hugely, it has the power to literally turn the tide so it's no surprise that it can affect the human body and energy system. You can use the energy of the moon to help you to release what no longer serves you and manifest what it is you want to attract. Once you have an awareness of the moon's cycle you can use her energy to magnify your intentions in lots of ways.

New Moon – this is when we see from earth mainly the darkness, as the moon is illuminated from the back. This darkness is a metaphor for the new beginning that is about to start, and for the blank canvas that we have the ability to seed our desires and intentions for the cycle that follows.

You can use the energy between a New Moon and a Full Moon to help draw in and magnify your intention.

Set a clear intention about what you want to draw in. Spend some time thinking about this and then write a list, remember that they need to be positive and in the present tense. You can supercharge this list by folding it and placing crystals on top, or putting it in a reiki box that you send energy to every day.

You can ask for Angelic help, or any other help from the universe that serves your highest good, but overall know that your intention and ability to align with the feelings that these experiences will bring are the most powerful ingredient.

If you want to have a New Moon ritual you can get centred and write your list with a candle burning and some incense filling the air, bringing any other aspects of spirituality into the mix that feel right for you such as drawing some oracle cards from a deck and asking for messages from your guides.

Once you have set your intentions remember to say thank you to the universe in advance for the experiences that are unfolding for you. If you want to you can bury your list in the ground under the light of the New Moon, with the intention of the earth nurturing and energizing your intentions to help them grow.

Full Moon – It is now that the moon is the brightest and it is when our emotions are mostly affected. This is a time when you can cleanse and supercharge crystals most effectively by placing them on a windowsill in the moonlight, or outdoors in contact with the earth.

Between now and the New Moon you are releasing.

The Full Moon is the time that you will know what you have been able to draw in and manifest, or at least what you have been able to start to manifest. Celebrate small victories, the universe hears this and sends you more. Say for example you were asking for financial abundance and you had a small unexpected windfall, it may not have been exactly what you wanted but you are still aligning with the flow.

Between now and the next new moon there is a time for releasing, this is an important part of manifesting what you want because not only does it make room in your life for more good stuff to come in, it helps you to stay mindful of how you may have been blocking your own flow and sabotaging yourself.

You can start making a list of everything that you want to release including self-sabotage, negative thought forms, unloving thoughts and behaviours and more. Forgive yourself as you write your list and others that you may be harbouring bad feeling about, and know that when the time comes for the New Moon you can start over by burning this list. Make sure you do this safely of course, and call to the Violet Flame to blaze through all aspects of you and everything on your list in order to transmute lower vibration energy into high vibration love and light.

Surviving a Mercury Retrograde

The planet Mercury governs truth, communication, travel, technology and clear thinking. Several times a year it goes into retrograde (which means it passes the earth and appears to orbit backwards). It's not really going backwards of course, but all of the above may feel as if they are for you for the retrograde period, as unexplained and crazy things tend to happen to us all.

Trains and flights get cancelled, someone misses a crucial email that you sent, you can't get through on a number to make an urgent call... the mess that Mercury makes for us can make us feel like we are on the verge of a breakdown and that the cosmic odds are stacked so high against us that we will never again get out of first gear.

And to top it all off there is a phenomena called a Retrograde Shadow, where typically two weeks before the stardust really hits the fan, you're already feeling it fly.

So what (on earth) can you do to help yourself through this?

Firstly, know that it's going to happen and avoid (if you can) starting anything new in the way of projects and assignments. Look after technology, back things up and make sure that you are super clear on all communication, think before you speak and be conscious of any texts or emails that you send at this time.

Don't over commit in your schedule, there is going to be some wiggle room needed at times. Be super careful about signing anything that is legal or relates to contracts, check and double check or wait if you can until after retrograde to sign them.

Do what you can to chill out and expect delays, when they hit, reach for the book or e-reader in your bag that you thought ahead to bring. Double check all travel arrangements, passport expiry dates and reservations.

Don't take everything personally, wires are commonly crossed and tempers flare at this time. Be super clear when giving and receiving information, make sure you don't jump to conclusions and you know what others actually mean.

And finally - make sure that you turn up the patience and tolerance, we are all going through this but some people won't know, at least you have a heads up!

Crystals

Crystals are helpful little vibrational power houses that can assist us in healing, releasing and manifesting. They all emit an energy that is a pure and constant frequency, and these frequencies have been known to help us in specific ways. The frequency that a crystal emits will entrain your energy system to align with it after a while, thus moving you away from chaotic energy patterns that create an unbalancing in our energy as well as physical and emotional symptoms, blockages etc.

You can use crystals in your energy field by putting them in a pocket or wearing in jewellery, you can have them under your pillow or on your bedside, or placed around a room to help clear and lift energy. When you are choosing a crystal, it's a good idea to have some awareness of what that crystal may be useful for, but don't buy based on this alone. Take the time to hold the crystal and feel the energy of it, let your intuition guide you and buy what you feel connected to, not just what is says in a book or online. Have an overall belief that the exact right crystal will find you at the right time when you need it, and then trust what comes onto your radar.

You may find that after working with a crystal for a little while that you lose or misplace it. This could be the universe passing it on to someone else that it needs to be with at the moment, or giving you an energetic break. Trust that this is happening in accordance with your highest good, and if it is lost hold the intention that whomever finds it will gain healing and positive benefits from it next.

Crystals absorb energy and therefore need to be cleansed regularly. You can do this by leaving them in the sunlight, the moonlight or running under water as long as they are not water soluble (selenite for example you can't). Once a month is usually about right but if you wear crystals this may need to be done more often.

I always like to test with a dowsing pendulum how much exposure I need to have to a crystal, with the intention that this is for my greatest and highest good. Never underestimate the power of these little gems, especially if you are energy sensitive. You may find you need to have a schedule to wear a pendant or bracelet, or that it's not appropriate to have a crystal under your pillow for more than a few nights.

You can also use crystals to grid a house, this will change the energy in the building and can help to raise the vibration and create a protective boundary around the property. Choose your crystals the usual way, by having some knowledge of what may be useful but also using your intuition. Using a dowsing pendulum can help you to see where you would need to place the crystals for the best possible outcome for all of the occupants. Beware of small children picking them up, a good way to avoid this is to plant them in a pot underneath a plant. This also lends the lovely earth energy to the crystal which they like to be immersed in, rather like going home for them.

Top Ten Crystals

Quartz – Amplifies energy, protects and brings extra energy to a person, room or situation.

Rose Quartz – Opens the heart chakra, facilitates self-love and helps love to blossom in relationships.

Amethyst – Known to reduce headaches, facilitate clear thinking and help you to open brow chakra.

Moonstone – Balances emotions and helps with intuition and fertility.

Haematite – Grounding and protective, helps overcome limitations and achieve goals.

Citrine – Energizing and uplifting, associated with prosperity and abundance.

Selenite – Connects us with our guides, dispels negative energy and protects.

Black Tourmaline – Super protecting from other people's energy, electromagnetics and more.

Carnelian – Physical and metal energy, decision making, creative projects and career.

Flourite – Spiritual and Psychic Protection – helps to ward off any negative energies and keep your aura clear.

Space Clearing

Our environment has a huge influence on the way we feel, and since emotions are energetic, the space we are in can change our vibration in positive or negative ways.

Everything is made up of energy, and this is never more evident than a cluttered environment. When there are lots of things around you and they are all radiating a different frequency, this can feel very jarring and uncomfortable. Some people that are very energy sensitive may get overwhelmed and emotional, or suffer anxiety in this type of environment.

A good clear out is often enough to lift the energy in a space, and if you have difficulty in doing this here is an idea you can try. First of all, know that you are only committing a set period of time to this task, whether that is ten minutes, half an hour or more, you choose. Set a timer and find something to listen to that makes you feel good. Know that whatever happens next you are doing your best.

Commit to making three piles, one is to throw away, one is to pass on to charity or goodwill and the third is to keep.

Start your timer and go for it!

See how much progress you make in the allotted time, and get some pace about it. When you move your body you change your state from stuck to taking action and the universe hears this, you will feel your vibration lift – if not during this process, then definitely at the end. Quite often, people keep going long after the timer because they are enjoying the feeling of clearing out what does not serve them.

Do this with the intention that you are letting go of what you no longer need, in order to make room for new positive opportunities and experiences. Have gratitude for the items that you are passing on or throwing away for their service to you so far in life, and release them with love.

If you find yourself getting stuck, stop and ask yourself "does this serve me right now?" and if the answer is no, find the pile it belongs to. Even a little progress using this method will help you to change the energy in your home and make you feel better, which in turn lifts your vibration and helps you to manifest more of what you want.

Once you have decluttered, some quick and easy ways to raise the vibration even more are as follows:

- Clap your hands in each corner of the room.
- Use bells or tone into the corners.
- Introduce more earth energy with plants and crystals.
- Ask that the space is flooded with Angelic light.
- Visualize the Violet Flame blazing through the room to transmute energy.
- Smudge with sage stick.
- Burn essential oils and essences.

Chakras

Chakras are the energy centres that draw in universal energy from the world around us and move it through all layers of our aura, our meridian system, and into our physical bodies. The word chakra comes from the Sanskrit word "wheel" because of the round shape and constant motion of these structures. There are seven main chakras in our human energy system, and each corresponds to a different aspect or part of us. They can become blocked because of past trauma, psychic attack or etheric cords from situations, places or people. When this happens you may experience symptoms related to that chakra in a physical, emotional, psychological or spiritual way depending on what is going on with you at the time. Here is a list of what each chakra relates to and some clues that will help you see if you are blocked in any way:

Crown Chakra – Top of Head - Violet

This relates to your connection to your higher self and All That Is. Think of it as cosmic broadband. This connects you to the universe, your guides and to the creative energy that we call God / Goddess Creator / Divine Director. If this chakra is blocked it is likely that you may not feel connected to your higher self, you may struggle to tune into your intuition and perhaps be getting bogged down in earthly drama instead of stepping back and raising your vibration above it.

"I AM connected to my Higher Self and All That Is."
Crystals – Selenite & Clear Quartz
Essential Oils – Lavender & Frankincense

Brow Chakra – Forehead – Indigo

This is the chakra of multidimensional awareness and perception, whereby you can tune into people and situations in a more sixth sensory way and work with your inner knowing and psychic abilities. Many of us close this down because we are fearful of what we might "see". Have an overall intention that you are only going to see or experience what is right for you at this time and in your highest good. Then you can release any fear knowing that you will not be able to access anything that could bring you harm. Remember that people tune into information in different ways, just because you do not vividly "see" does not mean that you are not receiving sixth sensory information. You may experience a knowing, or a feeling or even hear messages and insights. However information comes to you is right for you.

"I AM embracing my multidimensional awareness."
Crystals – Amethyst & Lapis Lazuli
Essential Oils – Juniper & Rosemary

Throat Chakra – Throat - Blue

This chakra is associated with authenticity and truth, it's about you being able to express your truth in your speech and in your behaviour. In other words be aligned with your real self, and show it. When this chakra becomes blocked, it is usually in situations where people are unable to be themselves or say how they feel. This can manifest as a clearing of the throat or cough, recurring throat infections and such. Sometimes this can be selective depending on which company you are in, for example you may be totally fine with your friends but when you are in the presence of a particular family member or colleague you always have an issue with your throat because you are in fear of them judging you if you are your real self. This is also a chakra where anger and resentment become stored, especially when you do not have a change to voice it.

"I AM safe to express my truth with love and grace."
Crystals – Blue Kyanite & Sodalite
Essential Oils – Eucalyptus & Chamomile

Heart Chakra – Chest – Green

This chakra is associated with love for others and for yourself. It is often closed down as a result of being hurt emotionally, but this can have a tendency to trap the trauma and pain within the chakra and stop you from processing and releasing it. If the time is not right for you to do this and the situation feels too raw, first of all be gentle with yourself and know that this will happen at the perfect time. Secondly, do what you can to get into the vibration of gratitude. Notice what you can in your everyday life that you can be thankful for and even when you feel really hurt, send thanks to the universe for the gifts in your life. This could be as simple as the food on your table, running water, your physical body, a sunny morning or a song on the radio. When you focus on what is good you can gently open your heart again with the intention of releasing those old wounds and healing at the right pace for you. Also look for ways that you can show yourself love and support yourself emotionally.

"I AM love in human form, my life reflects love back to me."
Crystals – Rose Quartz & Green Aventurine
Essential Oils – Rose & Ylang Ylang

Solar Plexus Chakra – Bottom of Rib Cage - Yellow

This chakra is associated with self-worth, self-image and self-confidence. This is the chakra that becomes blocked when we feel less than, or unworthy in any way. It's the one where we feel anxiety and a wobble coming on when we don't feel good enough in a situation or a relationship. It is really common for issues to arise in this area when we have had a knock in life, or a relationship has been unconscious or toxic and robbed us of our self-esteem.

"I AM worthy of all things good, simply for being me."
Crystals – Citrine & Yellow Jasper
Essential Oils – Black Pepper & Neroli

Sacral Chakra – Navel - Orange

This chakra is associated with sexuality and emotions and as such is commonly blocked or holding on to trauma from past relationships that have been challenging, toxic or unconscious especially if there has been sexual intimacy. There may be unprocessed feelings stuck in this energy centre that stop you from processing the relationship or its effect on you, and you may feel that there are wounds to heal around masculine and feminine issues and emotions. There could also be a pattern of emotional reactions because feelings have not been addressed and wounds are still raw.

"I AM emotionally healing and balancing in perfect time and order."
Crystals – Carnelian & Red Jasper
Essential Oils – Jasmine & Sandalwood

Base Chakra – Bottom of Spine - Red

This chakra is associated with us being grounded, present and connected to the earth. It is the chakra that gets blocked when we are fearful of being present on the earth and facing issues that are coming up for us, and is especially connected to money and flow. When we feel less than abundant this chakra stops its flow. It is also associated with the practicalities of living on earth and making sure that your basic needs are met such as food, shelter and warmth. If these are threatened in any way through a loss of income or a change in circumstances then this chakra is the one to close. This creates a huge issue because you can only work with Law of Attraction effectively if you are present, and when this chakra is blocked you cannot get grounded.

"I AM safe being present and grounded on the earth."
Crystals – Haematite & Black Tourmaline
Essential Oils – Geranium & Patchouli

Chakra Self-Healing

A simple and very powerful way to help your chakras to release stuck energy is to gather a crystal, an essential oil and the affirmation that you need for that chakra. Get grounded by visualizing your light cord travelling from your base chakra, down your legs and into the earth, ask that you are fully anchored and connected. Draw this energy up (simply through intention, don't worry if you don't feel anything) through your chakras and out of your crown, asking to be connected to All That Is. Now ask that all parts of you come in to the now time in order to receive this healing energy and to release old stuck wounds, lower vibration energy and anything that does not serve you.

Hold the crystal over the chakra in question with one hand and in the other hold the essential oil. Breathe in the scent of the oil and "send" the vibration with your intention to the chakra you are working on. Exhale and blow down your chakra column to the earth whilst thinking or saying out loud the corresponding affirmation. Repeat this 3 – 7 times, you may feel a tingling in your body as old energy leaves, or a wave of emotion. Intend that the energy is sent to the earth for recycling and give thanks for the lessons you have learned and the release you now draw in. You may want to keep the affirmation in your awareness for a few days in order to help the release process and to help integration of new positive vibrations as they come into your life. You can write it down and pin to a pin board, carry it in your purse or pocket, or simply memorize and use throughout the day. Likewise you can carry the crystal with you and use the essential oil in a burner to help you process.

What's on the Cards?

I love Oracle Cards and find them a great tool to help me connect with my higher self and my guides, to bring me confirmation and to help me to stay on my soul path. I have nothing against Tarot, I simply prefer Oracle Cards as I find them easier to use and read.

When choosing a deck of cards, trust your intuition and see what is calling to you. There are so many different kinds out there that you will be able to find something to suit, whilst holding the intention (and perhaps checking with a dowsing pendulum) which deck will work best with you. Don't give up if you get a deck of cards that you feel don't suit you, it may be that someone you know is manifesting some cards and they came to you in order to pass on! This has happened to me at least twice, don't give up just find the cards a new home and look for some more.

Once you have your lovely cards and you are ready to start working with them, a good way of starting is to hold each card in your left hand and look at it for a moment. The left hand is for reading and receiving energy, so you can ask that you are connected with the intention for that card and the messages that it holds. I like to place the card over my heart chakra next and read the description in the accompanying book for that card. I let the energy settle for a moment, I look at the card again, and then I return it to the deck and choose another.

Initially, and perhaps over a period of days I do this with every card. Please note that this is not to memorise each card, you will always have the guidebook, and if you want to go on to read cards regularly you will find after a while you don't need it. This is simply to set a clear intention with the universe that I am ready to work with the energy of these cards and the messages that they will impart to myself and others.

There are lots of different spreads that you can use, but I prefer to work intuitively and see how many cards I think I should draw at that time. You can do a card a day for yourself, or three cards at the beginning of the week for example, or a full six or twelve month spread. If in doubt I check with my pendulum and ask "how many cards do I need today?"

A word or warning, nothing is set in stone!

The universe is in a state of constant change and flux, and when you draw cards for yourself or others or when you have a reading from someone else, they are tuning in to the energy that is around you now and reading likely future possibilities based on the present. So often people unconsciously adapt their lives to mirror the detail in a reading, and then believe that by default the rest of the reading must be accurate. This is not always the case and a great opportunity for you to exercise discernment and also your own intuitive insights.

Trust your gut feeling, and use cards as another tool to help you in your life, but know that you always have freewill and that nothing is really set in stone.

THE ENERGY
OF MONEY

"Money is energy and can therefore be attracted like any other energy."

Kate Spencer

Money

Money is the name of the energy exchange that we use on earth, and it's something that we as healers, light workers, empaths and sensitive souls can get tied up in knots about. But why do we feel so uncomfortable?

This can be for several reasons, but at the root of all of them lie our beliefs about money. We all have a "money story" based on what we have learned from our lives and our experiences, and this is what drives our behaviour as well as our point of attraction.

Inherited Patterns

What was your parents' relationship with money like? Perhaps you were brought up in an environment where there was financial struggle and hardship, and the discussions and attitudes to money that surrounded you reflected this.

Our beliefs are formed early in our lives, and as we find evidence to support them, these beliefs become stronger. Maybe some of what you saw and heard as you were growing up has made you fearful of not having enough money, or judgmental about people who are abundant.

The thing to remember about our inherited patterns is that our parents lived in a completely different time and reality.

What was relevant then may not be now, and if we try to navigate through our lives using the old beliefs that we have absorbed through our upbringing, we could be sabotaging our progress in a big way.

For example if your parents were financially challenged, they may have viewed people that had money as greedy or snobby. This idea would have been generated from the lack that they felt, and associated emotions such as resentment and maybe even shame. If you happen to have integrated that belief into your own frame of reference, then there could be a part of you right now that is pushing your own prosperity away because you don't want to come across as being greedy.

Likewise if your parents had to work incredibly hard for all that they had, it's likely that you have some money beliefs that in order to generate an income you have to work incredibly hard.

This could set up behavioural patterns that sabotage parts of your life – for example, if you are so driven to work hard, you will miss out on family and friends, and work could well become your priority.

Another interesting thing about inherited beliefs is that often the person who imprints these beliefs onto you - in a well-meaning, this is how the world works kind of way - could well have had the same done to them in their formative years. They will be carrying around beliefs that their parents had been influential in creating, and then passed a version of these onto you, and of course the same will have happened to their parents and so on.

Many of the beliefs that you have may not be yours in the first place and may be so outdated that they are definitely not serving you in the world we live in now.

Cultural Concepts

A Mind Virus is a concept or an idea that catches on. Something that is spread from person to person quickly and accepted into their frame of reference before it's passed on again. Some Mind Viruses can be really useful such as the concept of recycling. When I was a kid I'm pretty sure that everything went in to one bin bag and there was no sorting paper, card, glass or metal to help the planet and ourselves. Now it's commonplace to see bins in public places that encourage you to separate rubbish, and we do it in our homes as well. Initially thought of by a person or group of people, this concept has now become the norm, and has spread globally. Local authorities caught on and businesses, the government gave incentives for recycling and so on. It's something we do, but it's also an example of a Mind Virus because as a concept it spread around a lot of people.

Other examples include Facebook, it's something that has caught on big style in our modern lives and most people that you connect with will either have an account or at the very least be aware that it exists. The latest fashion can be a Mind Virus (suddenly everyone I know has a Pug or the Pokemon Go app), it's any kind of concept that is passed from person to person and beds into your consciousness.

The very worst examples of concepts that have gripped humanity include the concepts associated with the Holocaust, which was started by one person's delusions of grandeur and hatred that combined with a position of power and influence and led to many people being influenced to do unspeakable harm to others. So what has this got to do with money?

The culture we are a part of in a broad sense, and the culture that we are a part of in terms of our social groups, will be influencing our money story. Think for a moment about how you see yourself in the world. Would you say you are doing well? Where would you say you were in a "class" system, if you believed one existed? How do you measure yourself against the rest of the world financially? And what beliefs have you absorbed about this along the way?

Examples of cultural beliefs about money may include the glass ceiling concept, women being paid less than men and the need to bolster up self-worth with designer merchandise. These beliefs are the ones that are created by the world we live in, the media and society in general. When you move even closer into your circle and the culture of your family and friends, you are likely to find that your money beliefs are in alignment with the people that you connect most with. We become like the people we spend time with, and our money beliefs are often no different.

If your money beliefs are very different to the people you are connected with in your circle of friends and family, it is likely that those you feel different to will irritate you when you talk about money. If you have healthy money beliefs you will find people with unhealthy beliefs very hard work and you may see them as being stingy, mean or self-sabotaging.

If you have unhealthy money beliefs you are going to find people in abundance as show-offs, who rub your nose in it and think they are better than you.

These examples are two opposing ends of the spectrum, but wherever you are on that scale you will find that whatever you think of other people and their money stuff is actually shining a light on your money stuff. The question is, now that you are aware of that are you going to do anything about changing it?

Your Attraction Field

Not only do limiting beliefs contribute to your day to day struggle in terms of money, they are also setting up the same pattern for the future. As long as you stay in your story of how things are with money, and how things should be, the more of the same experiences you will draw in. This will give you even more evidence that you are totally right, and your ego will love that kind of certainty.

"See? It's always been this way, and it always will be. People like me are never going to make it unless we win the lottery. And I don't want a big win mind, I don't want to be like those greedy buggers over the road with their new car every three years and their holidays abroad."

And so the pattern perpetuates, and so you get even more evidence, and so you stay well and truly stuck in your story and therefore your experience, because Law of Attraction continues to send you a match to what you are sending out. And you are so entrenched in your story that you expect it more and more, and draw it in at a rate of knots.

Observing other people's financial progress makes you resentful and adopt an attitude of "It's alright for them." This contributes to a mindset of "poverty consciousness" that is going to keep you absolutely stuck. You might not recognise yourself entirely in this picture, but if there is a part of your financial experience that you want to change, then there's a part of your story that you have to rewrite. That process starts with identifying the beliefs that you have about money.

What's your Money Story?

Dig deep and think about your money beliefs. What has your upbringing and life experience taught you about money so far? What are the thoughts and feelings that you honestly have about money?

- I believe

- I believe

- I believe

- I believe

- I believe

- I believe

- I believe

- I believe

- I believe

Even the process of just writing these beliefs down might make you start to question them. Let's take that a little further, ask yourself the following:

Is this mine?
Is this true?
Does this serve me?

The answers are likely to be a resounding no if your money experience is causing you frustration or pain in your life. Beliefs are formed by us gathering evidence to support them. As we have seen, often this evidence is presented to us by well-meaning people in our lives such as family and friends, and also by the media and the world we live in.

We accept this evidence and use it to prop up our belief, because as long as we can justify it to ourselves we can experience something called congruence. When we work on changing our beliefs it can feel uncomfortable, because the evidence that we thought was relevant and correct, can actually turn out to be stuff that we haven't really thought about and we have accepted on face value.

We have used these snippets of evidence to build the foundations to solid beliefs that actually turn out to be nothing more than a house built on sand once you are brave and honest enough to dig. And often the sad part is that these beliefs have been the bedrock for our life experience thus far. An example for me would be that I had a belief that it was super important to go to university, get a degree and then a "proper job". That was the only way that I was going to make any real sustainable money to support myself and a family. This was both an inherited belief and a cultural one at the time, and there was plenty of evidence for me to lay the foundations. Many of the adults in my life that were doing well financially had followed this path, having a degree was a benchmark of ability in most professional positions and the media told me that people who had graduated got paid more and had better prospects.

All of this information supported the belief that this was what I had to do in order to create a life with financial stability and success. So I did it. I landed my "proper" job in pharmaceutical sales, and just as I'd been promised the abundance flooded in.

It was about four years into this career that life blessed me with the most glorious gift, and I became a mother. There was simply no way that I could return to the demands of the job I had previously thrived on, and I went into panic. My beliefs were all set up to help me to be the person that I used to be, and I had no evidence to support the fact that I could leave corporate life and still be financially stable. This was a huge turning point for me, I knew that I couldn't go back to doing the job that I had, but I was so entrenched in my "proper job" story that I couldn't see any way forward.

The result was huge emotional stress and upset for me, until I could let go of those "proper job" beliefs that were holding me hostage. Luckily I was open minded enough (or scared enough?) to entertain the possibility that there could, maybe, be another way. I started to look at ways that I could maybe stay at home and work part time, and I also began to subconsciously gather evidence to support the new belief that was emerging. In the past when my beliefs were first formed, it would have been ridiculous to think that anyone could run a business from home using the internet and social media to make a good income.

I had no evidence of this working for anyone in my social sphere of influence at all. I latched on to the nearest feeling example and used the evidence that I could draw on to build a new belief and a new story and to help me model successful behaviour. And the turning point believe it or not was EBay!

This was a community where I could see lots of people working from home, online and making good money. The evidence was right there in front of my eyes. If they could do it then so could I. This evidence was used to shore up a new belief and send me in another direction entirely, and a one that led me to where I am today.

So now when I look at the belief that says, "You can only make a financial success of yourself in a proper job" I find that the evidence is not there for me.

Is this mine? No.
Is this true? No.
Does this serve me? Hell no.

What new beliefs do you need to create and what evidence can you use to support them? (The new belief could well be the opposite of the old one.)

- I believe

My evidence is:

- I believe

My evidence is:

- I believe

My evidence is:

- I believe

My evidence is:

- I believe

My evidence is:

It's probably a good time to bring up the concept of Worthiness, because if you feel unworthy of receiving then these statements will be really hard for you to create. Here's the thing - there is an endless supply of money and energy out there, fact. Imagine someone attaching a hose pipe to a tap and turning the water on full force. That's the flow of money and energy that you have access to, but your old beliefs are the equivalent of you standing on the pipe and pinching off the flow. You are totally worthy of lifting your foot up and allowing more goodness to flood into your life. No matter who you are, what you have been through and what other people have said to you. No matter how deep the scars, or how much you have messed up.

Today is the day that you can start over and you do not have to prove that worthiness to anyone. You're here. That sperm met that egg at the right time in history to make your body, and your soul chose this time and space and experience to grow and thrive. You've made it here against the odds, and now is the time to start to believe that you are worthy of creating a life that you love. And you are, I promise. I have a very strong intention at the time of writing this that the right people will read it, and if that's you then this message is lining up with that intention. If you have worthiness issues then please find a way to work on them, because they will be affecting everything - money included.

It's time to write your new money story, and attract a different experience. All of the new statements you have made can be formed into powerful affirmations starting with I AM. Read these affirmations to yourself every day and keep searching for and adding in more evidence that you know will support these new empowering money beliefs.

SELF CARE

"Give yourself and those you love the best version of you, by taking care of your precious self."

Kate Spencer

Tin Bucket Self Care

If you want to create a life that you love, then you have to be measured in where you "spend" your life force energy. Think of it as a valuable resource, like water. The universe gives you a monthly life force energy income, which we can break down into a weekly and daily average amount. You need some of this energy to fuel your regular day to day existence. Take a moment now to consider the energy that you have to spend within the first hour of getting up in the morning. Every task that requires your input is you spending your energy or life force, and that includes thinking and feeling as well as the practical. By the time you've had a shower, made coffee, dressed and left the house you've used up a percentage of your daily life force energy - but this isn't usually as straightforward in the real world.

Add into the mix a text message from an upset friend, a lost sports kit, a child's packed lunch to make, a last minute dash to the shop for bread, the television on in the background with a tragic breaking news story and more.... All of these things pull on our energy and either subtly or not so subtly deplete us of our energy before we even walk out of the door. Then there's the school run followed by the commute followed by finding a parking space and the walk into the office with the colleague that hates their job and their husband. You start to shore up your energy for the 9 to 5 and add in more coffee, which gives you a lift but steals a bit more of your energy as you start to come down in an hour's time. At break time you check your Facebook feed and see that someone has shared the recent news story that you tried to block out this morning, and the tragedy pulls you in again and you feel your energy drop. Whilst you're looking at your phone an email drops in from your kid's school about parents evening. You get a text message from your partner saying that they forgot that they were going out tonight to a meeting, apologies but won't be back in time to take your eldest to football, could you arrange something else. And you remember that you need cat food, milk and fabric conditioner so you make a note to go home via the supermarket, after dropping in to see if your parents need anything - after all they are on the way and you haven't seen them all week. Break time over, you head back into the lion's den and get on with the task at hand, you're so tired and it's only mid-morning..... Is it any wonder that we end up feeling exhausted and depleted a lot of the time? Our life force is constantly being sucked out of us in all directions, and in many cases we are so low on it that we don't know it's happening. We avoid looking at how wrung out we feel because we ironically don't have the energy to. But this is the only way that we can stop leaking our life force all over the place. Everyone has busy and stressful times in their life, I get that.

As I sit here and write these words I am nearly 18 months into a house renovation and boy have I felt it. Making decisions, co-ordinating tradesmen and moving furniture from room to room has been exhausting. Not to mention the fact that life cannot be put on hold - I've still had to show up as a parent, a wife, a daughter, a friend and in my work while this was going on, and that has at times left me overdrawn in my own life force account. I've hit the wall a couple of times and had to unplug altogether, handing the day to day running of my business over to colleagues temporarily and letting my friends know I was in lock down. Maybe that's what led me to write this, because I need to learn personally not to take it to the wire before I crash. I have thankfully never had full on burnout, but I have had a wobbly two weeks which I feel were a very close call this summer. So how on earth did this happen and why am I sharing?

Anyone who knows me knows that I am full on here to help other people. Those people might be the people out there in the world that read my books, look for card of the day on my Facebook page or glean something from my blog. If you bring it in a little closer, these are people in my work that connect within the conscious communities and programmes I build or as part of one to one coaching. Closer still are the group of people that I call friends, and closer again are my family. That's a lot of people and a lot of energy, and you will have a version of this in your life.

But it's good to help so many people, right? It's brave to follow your dream and get out there, isn't it? You need to answer that Calling don't you?

Yes, yes and yes. But here's the rub. Where on this list of people do you see me? Absolutely nowhere. And this creates an irony. You end up so energetically overdrawn that you can't give anymore. And you can't show up in the way that you used to. The people I want to be my best for, instead, get a half-arsed diluted version of who I can be, usually grumpy, tired and impatient. That's sad for me and for them. Now I'm not going to go all poor me here, because negative emotions and beating myself up cost even more energy. But what I am going to do is give you an analogy that you can apply to your life moving forwards. There are two things that you need to do in order to help yourself. One is to stop the life force energy leaking out of you, and the other is to replenish yourself more. Start seeing your life as a tin bucket, and imagine all of the energy drains in your life as holes in this bucket. Some may be bigger than others. Now in your mind's eye fill that bucket with the precious resource of water, which represents the life force energy that we all have flowing through us.

Take a deep breath, close your eyes and connect to yourself. Ask what these holes represent in your life. Are they people, situations, sabotaging behaviours or something different? Where is your energy being drained? And how can you plug the holes with love and light and an intention to stop the harm to yourself? It's important that you answer this from a self-care perspective, and if you are struggling you can reframe the question like this. "If I allowed myself to be really honest, who or what would these holes represent?"

Remember that no one else needs to know that you feel this way, you are not betraying anyone or being mean. Your focus is the opposite, it is on love and that love is being directed towards yourself. Once you have identified what it is that is draining your energy, you need to make a commitment to bung up the holes and stop your life force energy being so depleted. Ask yourself how you can move away from situations and behaviours that do not serve you. Do you need to stop staying up late and watching negative, drama driven drivel on the television? Do you need to stop spending time at the school gate being part of the gossip machine? Do you need to give up junk food or cut back on alcohol? Do you need to create better boundaries in personal relationships? Do you need to delegate a task or say "no" more often? Ask yourself what would a person who really embraced self-love do if they were in your position right now? Then start to create some action steps for yourself that will help you to make real life actual progress in this direction. Usually the hardest thing for us to do is to disconnect from people in our lives that drain our energy, especially if these are family members or colleagues. It's a much better idea to sidestep these people gradually and gracefully, rather than cutting off the connection suddenly. This is because it's likely to create far less drama, something they may like to thrive on, but equally something that will deplete you even more. Sidestepping can be done by deliberately creating a small amount of distance and better boundaries, and then gradually building on that with the intention that you are freeing you both from a situation that may have become toxic.

Know that if you are not in resonance with someone that they are not in resonance with you either and that this is ultimately right for both of you even if they don't know that at the outset. Once you have practiced plugging up the gaps you are ready to start looking for ways to increase your life force energy. What is it that fills you up? This is different for everyone, but examples could be spending time in nature, reading a novel, a bubble bath, a hobby or a massage. Whatever this is, it doesn't matter - what does matter is how you feel. When you feel good you are going to be topping up your life force energy, and this top up combined with reducing the outflow will mean that you start to feel so much better. And that feeling better will translate into you showing up better for yourself and the people that count, which in turn will make you feel even better and give you back a whole load of self-worth.

Soul Searching Questions

Things or people that deplete my life force energy:

What action I need to take to stop or reduce this (with love!):

Things that top up my life force energy:

How I am going to incorporate more of these into my life:

AKASHIC
RECORDS

"When we allow our soul to guide us, we are always shown the way."

Sue Krebs

Akashic Records

The Akashic Records are a concept that we as a collective have created, to show and represent a "place" where every thought, word, deed and intention is logged by the universe. In other words every single moment and feeling from every single being in every single lifetime is held there.

You can see why the Akashic Records are also sometimes called The Mind of God, as they are an all-encompassing vibrational account of all that has ever been. As a soul you have your own individual Akashic Record. As humans, the easiest way for us to conceptualize a large amount of data and information all being kept in one place is to consider this a huge archive or library of sorts. This is why we sometimes hear The Hall of Records being referred to as the place that our soul records are held.

Remember that this is a constructed concept for us to be able to get our human thoughts around the idea, and that actually there may not be one fixed place and space that does contain all of this information at the same time. Another name for this cosmic information hub is The Libraries of Light, and some people may have visited them in a quest for answers and insights.

I believe that our human brain creates a framework and idea that we can work with when we are in meditation or under hypnotic regression, a metaphor if you like, that helps us to understand the idea of a lot of information in one place and a piece of this information relating to every soul. This metaphor is what we have called The Akashic Records, and depending on how you process information as an individual and what you believe, you will experience The Akashic Records in a way that fits with you. By using the word "metaphor" I am not saying that this isn't real.

I am saying that this is the best way for our human mind and brain to understand the vastness of information that is out there inter-dimensionally, and that as such we have constructed this concept to help us to try to understand.

My experience of Akashic Records began when I studied to be a Life Between Lives practitioner. Based on the work of Michael Newton, this fascinating method of Soul Regression typically takes a subject back through their most recent past life and into the space "between lives".

Also referred to as the spirit world, or home. I had the amazing experience of visiting "The Library of Light" when in trance, and to me it looked and felt like a big old building with a vast and never ending interior lined with books on several floors. I was aware of other beings around me and when I was asked by my facilitator I said that these were beings that "worked" in the library.

Thoughts were telepathic and I was able to call to one of them to help direct me to my own record. When in trance I saw a large book being brought to me with my name scrolled over the front in gold italics. The book was white and when I opened it, I was able to connect with what looked like moving pictures and images of my life here on earth so far. When I touched an image I was drawn into it as an observer and I could see, feel and hear what was going on in that moment and scenario.

One of the most interesting things was that I could connect with what other people were feeling and thinking, which was very useful in giving me a different perspective on past occurrences. It is probably important to add here that just the same as any other spiritual work, you are going to get what is right for you at this time. If you embark on an Akashic journey, do so with the clear intention that what comes up for you is going to serve you in your life right now.

My soul didn't want to experience any of my past lives, and so they were not brought forwards in my records. Most people that I worked with when I was a practitioner did refer to past lives, and this was always an opportunity to mine for information that may be affecting them in the now in a conscious way with a healing intention.

Common reasons for people wanting to explore their records include why they may have chosen their family, partner or life path. Many of us are also curious about our purpose, calling and reasons for being here. Soul contracts are often brought up in discussion, as well as past life karma, how to heal from pain and trauma and how to create a life they love. And more often than not, people have lost someone close and they simply want to know that there is something else other than this human existence.

Soul Groups

Journeys into the Akashic Records can give you information about your Soul Group. These are the souls who you have incarnated with in this lifetime to help support, learn from and connect with.

Often you have incarnated with them in previous lifetimes (on earth or elsewhere) and you will often find that these are family members and close friends. It is common for members of a Soul Group to have an agreement or a sign so that when you meet up on earth you will know each other. This triggers in us as humans that feeling of familiarity when we meet a stranger, or an instant connection as if you have known someone before.

Often we find that the souls we are closely connected with in this lifetime may have been present in our past lives but had a different role, a parent may now be a child and vice versa. These choices can depend on what we wish to experience during that incarnation and also any lessons that we have agreed to learn for our soul's highest good, or any karma we have to work through.

Typically in a spiritual regression you will become aware of between twelve and fifteen members of your Soul Group, some of these may be people that you have not yet met on the earth plane.

Contracts

These are agreements that are made between souls before they come to earth. Typical Soul Contracts may be an arrangement to meet up and share a certain lesson, period of time or even to experience being together as a couple.

We all come to the earth to learn, grow and experience. Before we arrive in our physical form, it is common to discuss with our guides the lessons and experiences that we want to go through when we get here. These choices include things like our gender, our genetic families, life-changing moments and more.

It is important to mention here that there is a vast amount of information out there on this subject, and as with all of it I encourage you to take what you need.

Discernment is important in all aspects of life, but especially subjects like this. Just because something is written down and in print, does not make it true.

Be a truth seeker for yourself, set yourself on a quest to get as much information as you can and then see what feels right to you. I say this because the concept of choosing a body that may be less than perfect, or an earth life that includes hardship and struggle seems ridiculous to our human brain and ego.

I can dress it up as much as the next writer and say that we honour your journey, and that you are reflecting courage to the whole of humanity, but sometimes no matter how you pixie and unicorn it up some people are dealt a shit hand. You need to make sense of what you have been given, and you need to find out what it means to you.

No one has the right to tell you that you "chose" this, or that you had a contract for your ex-husband to treat you badly and then leave you for your best friend.

That said, I encourage you to look at your life from a Higher Self perspective. Step back from the human happenings and the day to day stuff that distracts us all away from the bigger picture of purpose and what it's all about. Get quiet, get into your heart and ask yourself what you came here for and why certain people are in your life, what have you come to teach them and share and vice versa. Call it contracts, luck, destiny or Law of Attraction. I believe that we are in each other's lives for a reason, and finding that out can be an incredible gift to us all.

Past Lives

Personally, I do believe in past lives. That's because I have been regressed and it felt very real to me. Before I'd had that experience I had a healthy curiosity but I wasn't completely sold.

I sometimes still wonder if the brain makes up a metaphor that helps us to piece together information in a tangible way, and we as humans believe this to be a previous incarnation. Let's say that even though I have experienced what I believe to be myself in former lives, that I can still be open minded and consider that this may not be "real", or rather my human and therefore third dimensional concept of real. There is a great deal of evidence from amazing people like Brian Weiss and Michael Newton who have documented thousands of case studies to show that there is something that happens, when we set an intention that we are going to look at our past lives. The interesting thing for me when I met Michael Newton was that although he is a very gentle, spiritual and noble man, he is also a scientist.

He was super clear on not leading a client with questioning and the use of clean language. I feel that this adds a great deal of weight and credence to his work, and I certainly consider him a highly ethical individual to work with. When someone that is as credible as this man gathers up a lot of information that points towards not only the concept of past lives to be valid, but also the between lives existence of souls and energy, then the subject suddenly has a genuine leg to stand on. If you are interested in this subject I highly recommend Michael Newton's books *Journey of Souls* and *Destiny of Souls*.

Future Lives & Experiences

As well as past information it is sometimes possible for you to glean future information and likely possibilities and life paths. This is because your current future is a vibrational match to who you are right now. You are sending out energy in this very moment that is drawing in a whole load of possible outcomes based on your vibration. As you change your thoughts and feelings in your present, you are influencing your vibration which changes likely possible future outcomes. Therefore future possibilities are very fluid and changeable.

You may find when you have access to your records that you can intend and draw in a glimpse or experience of likely future possibilities. These possibilities are showing you what may happen if you stay aligned and continue to release resistance to this outcome. It is important you remember however that these are exactly that - possibilities and not set in stone.

Accessing Your Akashic Records

You can work with a practitioner to access your records. Hypnosis is a frequently used tool for this and can be very helpful in getting you into the super conscious state that you need to connect.

Some people can relax deeply enough by using a guided meditation, and others may want to have their records read by someone here on the earth. This can happen much like a psychic reading or energy reading, and usually an Akashic Reader will want your full name, date and time of birth and they will complete their own journey or meditation into the Halls of Records and ask for your information. They can then channel this into a report for you and may want to email or speak to you in person about what they have found. If they are also a skilled energy worker they may be able to help you in your current life and circumstances by completing any cord cutting or similar things that you need at that time. As with all readings it is important to take what is in resonance with you.

Goodbye 2016

Closing off the previous year is important. It allows you the mental and emotional space and bandwidth to gain closure on what you need to carry over the learning and the gratitude, and to give yourself permission to start over.

A New Year is the beginning of a new cycle, and in order to embrace all of that lovely positive fresh start vibe, we need to say thank you and goodbye to what has gone before. This does not have to be an outwardly big thing, it can be a personal ritual that tells the universe that you are ready to step forward into the next part of your journey, with love, grace and New Year Mojo.

Light a candle, burn some incense and get some mood music on if you want to really set the tone. Do this your way, but even if you don't write anything down, give yourself the gift of thinking them through and knowing what your answers would be.

Profound Moments and Experiences:

Stuff I am Insanely Grateful For:

What I have learned:

How I have grown:

What I take forward with me:

What I need to leave behind:

What I need to forgive myself for:

And so it is:

Hello 2017! My New Story Starts Here

Every month you will have the chance to see what you need to review the month that has passed, work on consciously releasing what you need to, and realigning with what you want to create in your life experience. These moments at the beginning of the month will be really helpful for you, they are the stepping stones that pave the way to your big vision.

Speaking of which, what is it that you want to create this year for yourself?

How do you want your life to look in terms of relationships, health, income, spirituality, joy, happiness, family, career and more?

Let's start with getting some of your ideas down on paper so that you can really zone in on what you want to manifest, remember if your mind starts to butt in and give you all kinds of reasons why this stuff can't happen that this is your ego trying to sabotage you (and we all have one!)

Think of it this way, if you had the ability to create everything that you truly desire – what would that look like, sound like, taste like and most importantly feel like.

Write Your Story for the coming year in the present tense and create as much detail as you can. The more emotionally charged words and powerful language that you can use, the more feelings you will stir within yourself and the more easily it will be to send then out as a signal for the universe to match.

Here is an example to get you started....

I am loving the life that I live. Every day is brimming with abundance and health for me, my wellbeing flows so easily these days and I see it manifesting in my experience. I love that fact that I can eat food that nurtures my body and that I can experience a gorgeous hot shower every day. I feel so happy and connected to myself that it is easy to see how the universe keeps sending me so many opportunities to create more happiness and abundance in my life for me and my family. I can afford to be generous with others and this helps me to stay in fair exchange with all of the goodness I am receiving. I love the simple things in my life like fresh flowers and my garden, which is a metaphor for the way I am growing and evolving. I am surrounded by people that I love, and I feel it in every moment. My life is truly blessed and I know that this year it's just going to get even better. When I feel so blessed I know that the universe is going to send me even more and this makes me relax into being in the present.

You can put specific goals in your story such as you love having a luxury family holiday, or living in a home that you desire, or driving a car that you want to draw in – but be aware that when you feel really blessed and in the flow that these things come to you as a result of that.

Go ahead – write your big and awesome story for 2017!

Happy New Year
2017

"Don't count the days, make the days count."

Muhammad Ali

MY 2017 STORY

....

....

....

....

....

....

....

....

....

....

....

....

....

....

....

....

....

....

....

....

HELLO *January*

LIFE LESSONS...

"Some people come in our life as blessings, some people come in as lessons."

Mother Teresa

INTENTIONS IN ACTION

I AM *showing myself love this month by:*

....

....

I AM *nurturing relationships this month by:*

....

....

I AM *supporting my physical body this month by:*

....

....

I AM *honouring my spiritual path this month by:*

....

....

I AM *creating abundance for myself this month by:*

....

....

ATTITUDE OF GRATITUDE

This month **I AM** *in Gratitude for:*

....

....

....

....

....

....

....

....

....

....

....

....

....

....

....

....

....

....

MONTHLY MANIFESTATION

Positive, present moment and personal affirmations...

I AM . . . .

. . . .

I AM . . . .

. . . .

I AM . . . .

. . . .

I AM . . . .

. . . .

I AM . . . .

. . . .

I AM . . . .

. . . .

DECEMBER

26 *Monday*

Mercury Retrograde continues

Boxing Day

....

....

....

27 *Tuesday*

U.K Bank Holiday

....

....

....

28 *Wednesday*

....

....

....

29 *Thursday*

◯ **New Moon**

....

....

....

DECEMBER/JANUARY

Friday **30**

New Year's Eve

Saturday **31**

New Year's Day

Sunday **1**

JANUARY

2 *Monday*   \text{UK Bank Holiday}

....

....

....

3 *Tuesday*

....

....

....

4 *Wednesday*

....

....

....

5 *Thursday*

....

....

....

JANUARY

Friday 6

Saturday 7

Mercury Retrograde ends

Sunday 8

JANUARY

9 *Monday*

....

....

....

10 *Tuesday*

....

....

....

11 *Wednesday*

....

....

....

12 *Thursday*

● Full Moon

....

....

....

JANUARY

Friday **13**

Saturday **14**

Sunday **15**

JANUARY

16 *Monday*

....

....

....

17 *Tuesday*

....

....

....

18 *Wednesday*

....

....

....

19 *Thursday*

....

....

....

JANUARY

Friday **20**

Saturday **21**

Sunday **22**

JANUARY

23 *Monday*

....
....
....

24 *Tuesday*

....
....
....

25 *Wednesday*

....
....
....

26 *Thursday*   **Burns Night**

....
....
....

JANUARY

· ·

· ·

· ·

New Moon ◯

Chinese New Year

Saturday **28**

· ·

· ·

· ·

Sunday **29**

· ·

· ·

· ·

JANUARY/ FEBRUARY

30 *Monday*

....

....

....

31 *Tuesday*

....

....

....

1 *Wednesday*

....

....

....

2 *Thursday*

....

....

....

FEBRUARY

Friday **3**

Saturday **4**

Sunday **5**

THANK YOU JANUARY...
for your lessons, gifts and experiences

REVIEW...*What I learned and what I loved*

RELEASE...*What I need to forgive and forget*

RENEW...*What I need to focus on next month*

NOTES

BE PRESENT...

"For the present is the point at which time touches eternity."

C. S. Lewis

INTENTIONS IN ACTION

I AM *showing myself love this month by:*

....

....

I AM *nurturing relationships this month by:*

....

....

I AM *supporting my physical body this month by:*

....

....

I AM *honouring my spiritual path this month by:*

....

....

I AM *creating abundance for myself this month by:*

....

....

ATTITUDE OF GRATITUDE

This month **I AM** *in Gratitude for:*

....

....

....

....

....

....

....

....

....

....

....

....

....

....

....

....

....

MONTHLY MANIFESTATION

Positive, present moment and personal affirmations...

I AM ....

....

....

I AM ....

....

....

I AM ....

....

....

I AM ....

....

....

I AM ....

....

....

I AM ....

....

....

30 *Monday*

....

....

....

31 *Tuesday*

....

....

....

1 *Wednesday*

....

....

....

2 *Thursday*

....

....

....

FEBRUARY

Friday **3**

Saturday **4**

Sunday **5**

FEBRUARY

6 Monday

....

....

....

7 Tuesday

....

....

....

8 Wednesday

....

....

....

9 Thursday

....

....

....

FEBRUARY

Friday **10**

· ·

· ·

· ·

Full Moon ●

Saturday **11**

· ·

· ·

· ·

Sunday **12**

· ·

· ·

· ·

FEBRUARY

13 *Monday*

....

....

....

14 *Tuesday*   **Valentine's Day**

....

....

....

15 *Wednesday*

....

....

....

16 *Thursday*

....

....

....

FEBRUARY

Friday **17**

Saturday **18**

Sunday **19**

FEBRUARY

20 *Monday*

U.S.A Holiday - President's Day

....

....

....

21 *Tuesday*

....

....

....

22 *Wednesday*

....

....

....

23 *Thursday*

....

....

....

FEBRUARY

Friday **24**

Saturday **25**

New Moon ◯

Sunday **26**

FEBRUARY/MARCH

27 *Monday*

....
....
....

28 *Tuesday*

....
....
....

1 *Wednesday*

....
....
....

2 *Thursday*

....
....
....

MARCH

· ·

· ·

· ·

· ·

· ·

· ·

· ·

· ·

· ·

THANK YOU FEBRUARY...
*for your lessons, gifts
and experiences*

REVIEW...*What I learned and what I loved*

....

....

....

....

....

RELEASE...*What I need to forgive and forget*

....

....

....

....

....

RENEW...*What I need to focus on next month*

....

....

....

....

....

NOTES

HELLO
March

DISCERNMENT...

"You cannot change the people around you, but you can choose the people that you choose to be around."

Unknown

INTENTIONS IN ACTION

I AM *showing myself love this month by:*

....

....

I AM *nurturing relationships this month by:*

....

....

I AM *supporting my physical body this month by:*

....

....

I AM *honouring my spiritual path this month by:*

....

....

I AM *creating abundance for myself this month by:*

....

....

ATTITUDE OF GRATITUDE

This month **I AM** *in Gratitude for:*

....

....

....

....

....

....

....

....

....

....

....

....

....

....

....

....

....

MONTHLY MANIFESTATION

Positive, present moment and personal affirmations...

I AM ....

....

....

I AM ....

....

....

I AM ....

....

....

I AM ....

....

....

I AM ....

....

....

I AM ....

....

....

FEBRUARY/MARCH

27 Monday

....
....
....

28 Tuesday

....
....
....

1 Wednesday

....
....
....

2 Thursday

....
....
....

MARCH

Friday **3**

Saturday **4**

Sunday **5**

MARCH

6 *Monday*

....

....

....

7 *Tuesday*

....

....

....

8 *Wednesday*

....

....

....

9 *Thursday*

....

....

....

MARCH

. . . .

. . . .

. . . .

. . . .

. . . .

. . . .

Full Moon ⬤

. . . .

. . . .

. . . .

MARCH

13 *Monday*

14 *Tuesday*

15 *Wednesday*

16 *Thursday*

MARCH

St Patrick's Day   *Friday* **17**

. . . .

. . . .

. . . .

Saturday **18**

. . . .

. . . .

. . . .

Sunday **19**

. . . .

. . . .

. . . .

MARCH

20 *Monday*

....

....

....

21 *Tuesday*

....

....

....

22 *Wednesday*

....

....

....

23 *Thursday*

....

....

....

MARCH

Friday **24**

. . . .

. . . .

. . . .

Saturday **25**

. . . .

. . . .

. . . .

Mother's Day U.K

Sunday **26**

. . . .

. . . .

. . . .

MARCH

27 *Monday*

....
....
....

28 *Tuesday* ◯ New Moon

....
....
....

29 *Wednesday*

....
....
....

30 *Thursday*

....
....
....

MARCH/APRIL

Friday **31**

Saturday **1**

Sunday **2**

THANK YOU MARCH...
for your lessons, gifts and experiences

REVIEW... *What I learned and what I loved*

....

....

....

....

....

RELEASE... *What I need to forgive and forget*

....

....

....

....

....

RENEW... *What I need to focus on next month*

....

....

....

....

....

NOTES

HELLO
April

HEAL YOUR WOUNDS...

*"Although the world is full
of suffering, it is full also
of overcoming it."*

Helen Keller

INTENTIONS IN ACTION

I AM *showing myself love this month by:*

....

....

I AM *nurturing relationships this month by:*

....

....

I AM *supporting my physical body this month by:*

....

....

I AM *honouring my spiritual path this month by:*

....

....

I AM *creating abundance for myself this month by:*

....

....

ATTITUDE OF GRATITUDE

This month **I AM** *in Gratitude for:*

....

....

....

....

....

....

....

....

....

....

....

....

....

....

....

....

....

....

....

MONTHLY MANIFESTATION

Positive, present moment and personal affirmations...

I AM ....

....

....

I AM ....

....

....

I AM ....

....

....

I AM ....

....

....

I AM ....

....

....

I AM ....

....

....

MARCH

27 Monday

. . . .

. . . .

. . . .

28 Tuesday   ◯ New Moon

. . . .

. . . .

. . . .

29 Wednesday

. . . .

. . . .

. . . .

30 Thursday

. . . .

. . . .

. . . .

MARCH/APRIL

Saturday **1**

Sunday **2**

APPRIL

3 *Monday*

....

....

....

4 *Tuesday*

....

....

....

5 *Wednesday*

....

....

....

6 *Thursday*

....

....

....

APRIL

Friday **7**

....

....

....

Saturday **8**

....

....

....

Mercury Retrograde begins   *Sunday* **9**

....

....

....

APRIL

10 *Monday*

....

....

....

11 *Tuesday*   ● Full Moon

....

....

....

12 *Wednesday*

....

....

....

13 *Thursday*

....

....

....

APRIL

Good Friday

Friday **14**

....

....

....

Saturday **15**

....

....

....

Easter Sunday

Sunday **16**

....

....

....

APRIL

17 *Monday*

....

....

....

18 *Tuesday*

....

....

....

19 *Wednesday*

....

....

....

20 *Thursday*

....

....

....

APRIL

Friday **21**

Saturday **22**

Sunday **23**

APPLE

24 *Monday*

....
....
....

25 *Tuesday*

....
....
....

26 *Wednesday*   ◯ New Moon

....
....
....

27 *Thursday*

....
....
....

APRIL

Friday **28**

Saturday **29**

Sunday **30**

THANK YOU APRIL...
for your lessons, gifts and experiences

REVIEW...What I learned and what I loved

....
....
....
....
....

RELEASE...What I need to forgive and forget

....
....
....
....
....

RENEW...What I need to focus on next month

....
....
....
....
....

NOTES

HELLO

May

DRAMA QUEEN...

"Pour yourself a drink, put on some lipstick and pull yourself together."

Liz Taylor

INTENTIONS IN ACTION

I AM *showing myself love this month by:*

....

....

I AM *nurturing relationships this month by:*

....

....

I AM *supporting my physical body this month by:*

....

....

I AM *honouring my spiritual path this month by:*

....

....

I AM *creating abundance for myself this month by:*

....

....

ATTITUDE OF GRATITUDE

This month **I AM** *in Gratitude for:*

....

....

....

....

....

....

....

....

....

....

....

....

....

....

....

....

....

....

....

MONTHLY MANIFESTATION

Positive, present moment and personal affirmations...

I AM..

....

....

I AM..

....

....

I AM..

....

....

I AM..

....

....

I AM..

....

....

I AM..

....

....

MAY

1 *Monday*   U.K Bank Holiday

....
....
....

2 *Tuesday*

....
....
....

3 *Wednesday*   **Mercury Retrograde ends**

....
....
....

4 *Thursday*

....
....
....

MAY

Saturday **6**

Sunday **7**

MAY

8 *Monday*

. . . .

. . . .

. . . .

9 *Tuesday*

. . . .

. . . .

. . . .

10 *Wednesday*   ● Full Moon

. . . .

. . . .

. . . .

11 *Thursday*

. . . .

. . . .

. . . .

MAY

Friday **12**

Saturday **13**

Mother's Day U.S.A, Australia & N.Z

Sunday **14**

MAY

15 *Monday*

· ·

· ·

· ·

16 *Tuesday*

· ·

· ·

· ·

17 *Wednesday*

· ·

· ·

· ·

18 *Thursday*

· ·

· ·

· ·

MAY

Friday **19**

Saturday **20**

Sunday **21**

MAY

22 Monday

....

....

....

23 Tuesday

....

....

....

24 Wednesday

....

....

....

25 Thursday   ◯ New Moon

....

....

....

MAY

· ·

· ·

· ·

Saturday **27**

· ·

· ·

· ·

Sunday **28**

· ·

· ·

· ·

MAY/JUNE

29 *Monday*   **U.K Bank Holiday**
                                                       Memorial Day

· ·

· ·

· ·

30 *Tuesday*

· ·

· ·

· ·

31 *Wednesday*

· ·

· ·

· ·

1 *Thursday*

· ·

· ·

· ·

JUNE

THANK YOU MAY...
for your lessons, gifts
and experiences

REVIEW... *What I learned and what I loved*

....

....

....

....

....

RELEASE... *What I need to forgive and forget*

....

....

....

....

....

RENEW... *What I need to focus on next month*

....

....

....

....

....

NOTES

HELLO

June

BURDENS...

"Let go or be dragged."

Zen Proverb

INTENTIONS IN ACTION

I AM *showing myself love this month by:*

....

....

I AM *nurturing relationships this month by:*

....

....

I AM *supporting my physical body this month by:*

....

....

I AM *honouring my spiritual path this month by:*

....

....

I AM *creating abundance for myself this month by:*

....

....

ATTITUDE OF GRATITUDE

This month **I AM** *in Gratitude for:*

....

....

....

....

....

....

....

....

....

....

....

....

....

....

....

....

....

....

MONTHLY MANIFESTATION

Positive, present moment and personal affirmations...

I AM ....

....

....

I AM ....

....

....

I AM ....

....

....

I AM ....

....

....

I AM ....

....

....

I AM ....

....

....

MAY/JUNE

29 *Monday*

U.K Bank Holiday
Memorial Day

· ·

· ·

· ·

30 *Tuesday*

· ·

· ·

· ·

31 *Wednesday*

· ·

· ·

· ·

1 *Thursday*

· ·

· ·

· ·

JUNE

Friday **2**

. . . .

. . . .

. . . .

Saturday **3**

. . . .

. . . .

. . . .

Sunday **4**

. . . .

. . . .

. . . .

JUNE

5 *Monday*

....

....

....

6 *Tuesday*

....

....

....

7 *Wednesday*

....

....

....

8 *Thursday*

....

....

....

JUNE

Friday **9**

· ·

· ·

· ·

Saturday **10**

· ·

· ·

· ·

Sunday **11**

· ·

· ·

· ·

JUNE

12 *Monday*

....

....

....

13 *Tuesday*

....

....

....

14 *Wednesday*

....

....

....

15 *Thursday*

....

....

....

JUNE

Friday **16**

Saturday **17**

Father's Day U.K & U.S.A

Sunday **18**

JUNE

19 *Monday*

....
....
....

20 *Tuesday*

....
....
....

21 *Wednesday*

....
....
....

22 *Thursday*

....
....
....

JUNE

Friday **23**

....

....

....

New Moon ◯

Saturday **24**

....

....

....

Sunday **25**

....

....

....

JUNE

26 *Monday*

....

....

....

27 *Tuesday*

....

....

....

28 *Wednesday*

....

....

....

29 *Thursday*

....

....

....

JUNE/JULY

Friday **30**

....

....

....

Saturday **1**

....

....

....

Sunday **2**

....

....

....

THANK YOU JUNE...
for your lessons,
gifts and
experiences

REVIEW...*What I learned and what I loved*

RELEASE...*What I need to forgive and forget*

RENEW...*What I need to focus on next month*

NOTES

HELLO
July

PSYCHIC ATTACK...

"Fools take a knife and stab people in the back. The wise take a knife, cut the cord and free themselves from the fools."

Unknown

INTENTIONS IN ACTION

I AM *showing myself love this month by:*

....

....

I AM *nurturing relationships this month by:*

....

....

I AM *supporting my physical body this month by:*

....

....

I AM *honouring my spiritual path this month by:*

....

....

I AM *creating abundance for myself this month by:*

....

....

ATTITUDE OF GRATITUDE

This month **I AM** *in Gratitude for:*

MONTHLY MANIFESTATION

Positive, present moment and personal affirmations...

I AM . . . .

. . . .

. . . .

I AM . . . .

. . . .

. . . .

I AM . . . .

. . . .

. . . .

I AM . . . .

. . . .

. . . .

I AM . . . .

. . . .

. . . .

I AM . . . .

. . . .

. . . .

JUNE

26 *Monday*

....

....

....

27 *Tuesday*

....

....

....

28 *Wednesday*

....

....

....

29 *Thursday*

....

....

....

JUNE/JULY

Friday **30**

Saturday **1**

Sunday **2**

JULY

3 *Monday*

....

....

....

4 *Tuesday*   **U.S.A Holiday - Independence Day**

....

....

....

5 *Wednesday*

....

....

....

6 *Thursday*

....

....

....

JULY

Friday **7**

Saturday **8**

Full Moon ● Sunday **9**

JULY

10 *Monday*

....

....

....

11 *Tuesday*

....

....

....

12 *Wednesday*

....

....

....

13 *Thursday*

....

....

....

JULY

Friday **14**

Saturday **15**

Sunday **16**

JULY

17 *Monday*

. . . .

. . . .

. . . .

18 *Tuesday*

. . . .

. . . .

. . . .

19 *Wednesday*

. . . .

. . . .

. . . .

20 *Thursday*

. . . .

. . . .

. . . .

JULY

Friday **21**

Saturday **22**

New Moon ◯   Sunday **23**

JULY

24 *Monday*

....
....
....

25 *Tuesday*

....
....
....

26 *Wednesday*

....
....
....

27 *Thursday*

....
....
....

JULY

Friday **28**

. . . .

. . . .

. . . .

Saturday **29**

. . . .

. . . .

. . . .

Sunday **30**

. . . .

. . . .

. . . .

JULY/AUGUST

31 *Monday*

....

....

....

1 *Tuesday*

....

....

....

2 *Wednesday*

....

....

....

3 *Thursday*

....

....

....

AUGUST

THANK YOU JULY...
*for your
lessons,
gifts and
experiences*

REVIEW...*What I learned and what I loved*

....

....

....

....

....

RELEASE...*What I need to forgive and forget*

....

....

....

....

....

RENEW...*What I need to focus on next month*

....

....

....

....

....

NOTES

HELLO
August

NURTURE
YOUR BODY...

"Take care of
your body, it's the
only place you have
to live in."

Jim Rohn

INTENTIONS IN ACTION

I AM *showing myself love this month by:*

....

....

I AM *nurturing relationships this month by:*

....

....

I AM *supporting my physical body this month by:*

....

....

I AM *honouring my spiritual path this month by:*

....

....

I AM *creating abundance for myself this month by:*

....

....

ATTITUDE OF GRATITUDE

This month **I AM** *in Gratitude for:*

MONTHLY MANIFESTATION

Positive, present moment and personal affirmations...

I AM ....

....

....

I AM ....

....

....

I AM ....

....

....

I AM ....

....

....

I AM ....

....

....

I AM ....

....

....

JULY/AUGUST

31 *Monday*

....

....

....

1 *Tuesday*

....

....

....

2 *Wednesday*

....

....

....

3 *Thursday*

....

....

....

AUGUST

Friday **4**

Saturday **5**

Sunday **6**

AUGUST

7 *Monday*   ● **Full Moon**

....

....

....

8 *Tuesday*

....

....

....

9 *Wednesday*

....

....

....

10 *Thursday*

....

....

....

AUGUST

Friday **11**

· ·

· ·

· ·

Mercury Retrograde begins   *Saturday* **12**

· ·

· ·

· ·

Sunday **13**

· ·

· ·

· ·

AUGUST

14 *Monday*

....

....

....

15 *Tuesday*

....

....

....

16 *Wednesday*

....

....

....

17 *Thursday*

....

....

....

AUGUST

Friday **18**

· ·

· ·

· ·

Saturday **19**

· ·

· ·

· ·

Sunday **20**

· ·

· ·

· ·

AUGUST

21 *Monday* ⬭ New Moon

. . . .

. . . .

. . . .

22 *Tuesday*

. . . .

. . . .

. . . .

23 *Wednesday*

. . . .

. . . .

. . . .

24 *Thursday*

. . . .

. . . .

. . . .

AUGUST

Friday **25**

Saturday **26**

Sunday **27**

AUGUST

28 Monday

U.K Bank Holiday

....

....

....

29 Tuesday

....

....

....

30 Wednesday

....

....

....

31 Thursday

....

....

....

SEPTEMBER

Friday 1

Saturday 2

Sunday 3

THANK YOU
AUGUST...
*for your
lessons, gifts
and experiences*

REVIEW...*What I learned and what I loved*

RELEASE...*What I need to forgive and forget*

RENEW...*What I need to focus on next month*

NOTES

HELLO
September

BELIEVE IN MIRACLES...

*"I am realistic,
I expect miracles."*

Dr Wayne Dyer

INTENTIONS IN ACTION

I AM *showing myself love this month by:*

....
....

I AM *nurturing relationships this month by:*

....
....

I AM *supporting my physical body this month by:*

....
....

I AM *honouring my spiritual path this month by:*

....
....

I AM *creating abundance for myself this month by:*

....
....

ATTITUDE OF GRATITUDE

This month **I AM** *in Gratitude for:*

....

....

....

....

....

....

....

....

....

....

....

....

....

....

....

....

....

....

....

MONTHLY MANIFESTATION

Positive, present moment and personal affirmations...

I AM ....

....

....

I AM ....

....

....

I AM ....

....

....

I AM ....

....

....

I AM ....

....

....

I AM ....

....

....

AUGUST

28 *Monday*   **U.K Bank Holiday**

....

....

....

29 *Tuesday*

....

....

....

30 *Wednesday*

....

....

....

31 *Thursday*

....

....

....

SEPTEMBER

Friday **1**

....

....

....

Saturday **2**

....

....

....

Sunday **3**

....

....

....

SEPTEMBER

4 *Monday*   U.S.A Holiday - Labor Day

....
....
....

5 *Tuesday*   **Mercury Retrograde ends**

....
....
....

6 *Wednesday*   ● Full Moon

....
....
....

7 *Thursday*

....
....
....

SEPTEMBER

Friday **8**

Saturday **9**

Sunday **10**

SEPTEMBER

11 *Monday*

....

....

....

12 *Tuesday*

....

....

....

13 *Wednesday*

....

....

....

14 *Thursday*

....

....

....

SEPTEMBER

Friday **15**

Saturday **16**

Sunday **17**

SEPTEMBER

18 *Monday*

....
....
....

19 *Tuesday*

....
....
....

20 *Wednesday*   ◯ New Moon

....
....
....

21 *Thursday*

....
....
....

SEPTEMBER

Friday **22**

Saturday **23**

Sunday **24**

SEPTEMBER

25 *Monday*

....

....

....

26 *Tuesday*

....

....

....

27 *Wednesday*

....

....

....

28 *Thursday*

....

....

....

SEPTEMBER/OCTOBER

Friday **29**

· ·

· ·

· ·

Saturday **30**

· ·

· ·

· ·

Sunday **1**

· ·

· ·

· ·

THANK YOU SEPTEMBER...

*for your lessons, gifts
and experiences*

REVIEW...What I learned and what I loved

....

....

....

....

....

RELEASE...What I need to forgive and forget

....

....

....

....

....

RENEW...What I need to focus on next month

....

....

....

....

....

NOTES

HELLO
October

BETRAYAL...

"Sometimes the person you would take a bullet for, ends up being the person behind the trigger."

Taylor Swift

INTENTIONS IN ACTION

I AM *showing myself love this month by:*

....

....

I AM *nurturing relationships this month by:*

....

....

I AM *supporting my physical body this month by:*

....

....

I AM *honouring my spiritual path this month by:*

....

....

I AM *creating abundance for myself this month by:*

....

....

ATTITUDE OF GRATITUDE

This month **I AM** *in Gratitude for:*

....

....

....

....

....

....

....

....

....

....

....

....

....

....

....

....

....

....

MONTHLY MANIFESTATION

Positive, present moment and personal affirmations...

I AM . . . .

. . . .

. . . .

I AM . . . .

. . . .

. . . .

I AM . . . .

. . . .

. . . .

I AM . . . .

. . . .

. . . .

I AM . . . .

. . . .

. . . .

I AM . . . .

. . . .

. . . .

SEPTEMBER

25 Monday

....

....

....

26 Tuesday

....

....

....

27 Wednesday

....

....

....

28 Thursday

....

....

....

SEPTEMBER/OCTOBER

Friday **29**

....

....

....

Saturday **30**

....

....

....

Sunday **1**

....

....

....

OCTOBER

2 *Monday*

. . . .

. . . .

. . . .

3 *Tuesday*

. . . .

. . . .

. . . .

4 *Wednesday*

. . . .

. . . .

. . . .

5 *Thursday*   ● Full Moon

. . . .

. . . .

. . . .

OCTOBER

Friday **6**

Saturday **7**

Sunday **8**

OCTOBER

9 *Monday*   U.S.A Holiday (some States) - Columbus Day

....

....

....

10 *Tuesday*

....

....

....

11 *Wednesday*

....

....

....

12 *Thursday*

....

....

....

OCTOBER

Friday **13**

Saturday **14**

Sunday **15**

OCTOBER

16 *Monday*

17 *Tuesday*

18 *Wednesday*

19 *Thursday* ◯ New Moon

OCTOBER

Friday **20**

···
···
···

Saturday **21**

···
···
···

Sunday **22**

···
···
···

OCTOBER

23 *Monday*

....

....

....

24 *Tuesday*

....

....

....

25 *Wednesday*

....

....

....

26 *Thursday*

....

....

....

OCTOBER

Friday **27**

Saturday **28**

Sunday **29**

OCTOBER/NOVEMBER

30 *Monday*

....
....
....

31 *Tuesday*   **Halloween**

....
....
....

1 *Wednesday*

....
....
....

2 *Thursday*

....
....
....

NOVEMBER

....

....

....

Full Moon ●

....

....

....

....

....

....

THANK YOU
OCTOBER...
for your
lessons,
gifts and
experiences

REVIEW...*What I learned and what I loved*

. . . .

. . . .

. . . .

. . . .

. . . .

RELEASE...*What I need to forgive and forget*

. . . .

. . . .

. . . .

. . . .

. . . .

RENEW...*What I need to focus on next month*

. . . .

. . . .

. . . .

. . . .

. . . .

NOTES

HELLO
November

SOUL PATH...

"You are the universe
expressing itself as a human
for a little while."

Erkhart Tolle

INTENTIONS IN ACTION

I AM *showing myself love this month by:*

....

....

I AM *nurturing relationships this month by:*

....

....

I AM *supporting my physical body this month by:*

....

....

I AM *honouring my spiritual path this month by:*

....

....

I AM *creating abundance for myself this month by:*

....

....

ATTITUDE OF GRATITUDE

This month **I AM** *in Gratitude for:*

....

....

....

....

....

....

....

....

....

....

....

....

....

....

....

....

....

....

MONTHLY MANIFESTATION

Positive, present moment and personal affirmations...

I AM ....

....

....

I AM ....

....

....

I AM ....

....

....

I AM ....

....

....

I AM ....

....

....

I AM ....

....

....

OCTOBER/NOVEMBER

30 *Monday*

....

....

....

31 *Tuesday*   **Halloween**

....

....

....

1 *Wednesday*

....

....

....

2 *Thursday*

....

....

....

NOVEMBER

Friday **3**

· ·

· ·

· ·

Full Moon ●

Saturday **4**

· ·

· ·

· ·

Sunday **5**

· ·

· ·

· ·

NOVEMBER

6 *Monday*

....
....
....

7 *Tuesday*

....
....
....

8 *Wednesday*

....
....
....

9 *Thursday*

....
....
....

NOVEMBER

Friday **10**

U.S.A Holiday - Veteran's Day

Saturday **11**

Sunday **12**

NOVEMBER

13 *Monday*

14 *Tuesday*

15 *Wednesday*

16 *Thursday*

NOVEMBER

Friday **17**

New Moon ◯

Saturday **18**

Sunday **19**

NOVEMBER

20 *Monday*

....
....
....

21 *Tuesday*

....
....
....

22 *Wednesday*

....
....
....

23 *Thursday*   **U.S.A Holiday - Thanksgiving Day**

....
....
....

NOVEMBER

Friday **24**

. . . .

. . . .

. . . .

Saturday **25**

. . . .

. . . .

. . . .

Sunday **26**

. . . .

. . . .

. . . .

NOVEMBER

27 *Monday*

....

....

....

28 *Tuesday*

....

....

....

29 *Wednesday*

....

....

....

30 *Thursday*

....

....

....

DECEMBER

Friday 1

Mercury Retrograde begins

Saturday 2

Full Moon ●

Sunday 3

THANK YOU
NOVEMBER...

*for your lessons, gifts
and experiences*

REVIEW...*What I learned and what I loved*

....

....

....

....

....

RELEASE...*What I need to forgive and forget*

....

....

....

....

....

RENEW...*What I need to focus on next month*

....

....

....

....

....

NOTES

YOUR MESSAGE TO THE WORLD...

"Your life is your message to the world, make sure it's inspiring."

Unknown

INTENTIONS IN ACTION

I AM showing myself love this month by:

. . . .

. . . .

I AM nurturing relationships this month by:

. . . .

. . . .

I AM supporting my physical body this month by:

. . . .

. . . .

I AM honouring my spiritual path this month by:

. . . .

. . . .

I AM creating abundance for myself this month by:

. . . .

. . . .

ATTITUDE OF GRATITUDE

This month **I AM** in Gratitude for:

MONTHLY MANIFESTATION

Positive, present moment and personal affirmations...

I AM . . . .

. . . .

. . . .

I AM . . . .

. . . .

. . . .

I AM . . . .

. . . .

. . . .

I AM . . . .

. . . .

. . . .

I AM . . . .

. . . .

. . . .

I AM . . . .

. . . .

. . . .

NOVEMBER

27 *Monday*

28 *Tuesday*

29 *Wednesday*

30 *Thursday*

DECEMBER

Friday **1**

. . . .

. . . .

. . . .

Mercury Retrograde begins

Saturday **2**

. . . .

. . . .

. . . .

Full Moon ●

Sunday **3**

. . . .

. . . .

. . . .

DECEMBER

4 *Monday*

....
....
....

5 *Tuesday*

....
....
....

6 *Wednesday*

....
....
....

7 *Thursday*

....
....
....

DECEMBER

Friday **8**

Saturday **9**

Sunday **10**

DECEMBER

11 *Monday*

....

....

....

12 *Tuesday*

....

....

....

13 *Wednesday*

....

....

....

14 *Thursday*

....

....

....

DECEMBER

Friday **15**

· ·

· ·

· ·

Saturday **16**

· ·

· ·

· ·

Sunday **17**

· ·

· ·

· ·

DECEMBER

18 *Monday* ◯ New Moon

. . . .

. . . .

. . . .

19 *Tuesday*

. . . .

. . . .

. . . .

20 *Wednesday*

. . . .

. . . .

. . . .

21 *Thursday*

. . . .

. . . .

. . . .

DECEMBER

Mercury Retrograde ends

Friday **22**

Saturday **23**

Christmas Eve

Sunday **24**

DECEMBER

25 *Monday*   Christmas Day

· ·

· ·

· ·

26 *Tuesday*   Boxing Day

· ·

· ·

· ·

27 *Wednesday*

· ·

· ·

· ·

28 *Thursday*

· ·

· ·

· ·

DECEMBER

· ·

· ·

· ·

· ·

· ·

· ·

New Year's Eve

· ·

· ·

· ·

THANK YOU DECEMBER...
for your lessons,
gifts and
experiences

REVIEW...What I learned and what I loved

....

....

....

....

....

RELEASE...What I need to forgive and forget

....

....

....

....

....

RENEW...What I need to focus on next month

....

....

....

....

....

"Endings are really just new beginnings."

~ Love Kate x

Goodbye and
THANK YOU
2017

Acknowledgements

A BIG thank you to my design team...

Michelle Emerson, content edit & typeset
~ www.thewritersassistant.co.uk

Leanne Kelly, diary & graphic design
~ www.facebook.com/Jakenna.creative.design

Simon Avery, cover design
~ www.idobookcovers.com

Photography by Sarah Loveland
~ www.sarahloveland.com

www.kate-spencer.com

My gift to you...
Download your free meditation bundle here:
www.kate-spencer.com/the-journal-journey

CPSIA information can be obtained
at www.ICGtesting.com
Printed in the USA
BVOW10s0602030117
472343BV00033B/109/P